I0560945

EXPLORING THE LIVES OF WOMEN IN THE BIBLE

FAITH-BUILDING INSIGHTS AND PRACTICAL
LESSONS ANYONE CAN USE FOR TODAY'S
CHALLENGES

VOLUME 1

HOPE MAREN

© **Copyright 2025 - All rights reserved.**

The content within this book may not be reproduced, duplicated or transmitted without direct written permission from the author or the publisher.

Under no circumstances will any blame or legal responsibility be held against the publisher, or author, for any damages, reparation, or monetary loss due to the information contained within this book. Either directly or indirectly. You are responsible for your own choices, actions, and results.

Legal Notice:

This book is copyright protected. This book is only for personal use. You cannot amend, distribute, sell, use, quote or paraphrase any part, of the content within this book, without the consent of the author or publisher.

Disclaimer Notice:

Please note the information contained within this document is for educational and entertainment purposes only. All effort has been expended to present accurate, up-to-date, and reliable, complete information. No warranties of any kind are declared or implied. Readers acknowledge that the author is not engaging in the rendering of legal, financial, medical or professional advice. The content within this book has been derived from various sources. Please consult a licensed professional before attempting any techniques outlined in this book.

By reading this document, the reader agrees that under no circumstances is the author responsible for any losses, direct or indirect, which are incurred as a result of the use of the information contained within this document, including, but not limited to, — errors, omissions, or inaccuracies.

CONTENTS

INTRODUCTION

There was a moment, not too long ago, when I found myself in the kitchen, hands deep in soapy water, pondering the story of Esther. The queen who faced a king with a fierce courage I could only dream of. I wondered what she would say to a woman like me—a woman juggling life's endless demands while trying to hear God's whispers amid the chaos. Esther's story, like so many others in the Bible, holds a mirror to our own lives. It's a reminder that the challenges faced by women thousands of years ago still echo in our hearts today.

Exploring the various women of the Bible has taught me much and encouraged me on my faith journey. There are many women in the Bible who have something to say or teach us—so many that I share their stories over two volumes.

The purpose of these books is simple yet profound. It is to travel alongside these women in the Bible, gleaning faith-building insights and practical lessons. These lessons are not confined to ancient times but are alive and breathing, ready to help us navigate today's struggles. Whether it's finding the courage to speak up or nurturing love in the middle of conflict, these stories offer us a roadmap.

To you, dear reader, a woman of faith, a seeker of truth—I see you. I know the longing for a deeper connection to the stories that shaped our faith, the desire to grow, to find strength when it feels like you're running on empty. This book is for you to help you see that you're not alone. The women of the Bible walked this path before us, and their stories are here to guide us.

What makes these volumes unique? They include more than just the stories of well-known figures like Ruth or Mary. We'll also explore the lives of lesser-known women whose stories hold just as much power. Each profile includes historical context and reflection questions—our "Deeper Insight" moments—to help you engage in a personal dialogue with these narratives.

What can you expect? You can expect a journey to increase your faith and offer personal validation. It will provide practical strategies to manage today's challenges drawn from the timeless wisdom of these biblical women. You'll find chapters dedicated to courage, leadership, love, and resilience. Each chapter contributes to an overarching narrative of strength and faith.

In this volume, you will meet women like Eve, whose choices shaped humanity's story yet who still stands as a reminder of God's grace. You'll encounter Sarah, who teaches us that even in seasons of waiting, God's promises never fail. You'll walk with Hagar, a woman who found God's presence in the wilderness, proving that no one is forgotten or unseen.

You'll also be inspired by women who modeled incredible courage, like Shiphrah and Puah, who defied injustice to save innocent lives, and Deborah, a wise and fearless leader who trusted God's guidance. Through stories of steadfast love, like Ruth's unwavering devotion and Abigail's peacemaking wisdom, you'll see how relationships rooted in faith can shape futures.

As you read each chapter, please feel free to explore each story further by reading along. I used an online version of the NIV Bible, Bible Gateway. (n.d.). *Bible Gateway*. https://www.bible gateway.com/. You can search for specific passages and chapters very easily. The site also offers a daily Bible verse and a monthly membership if you wish to explore the Bible more in-depth.

These books also reflect my own journey. My passion for helping women connect with the Bible's women stems from my own struggles and triumphs. I've walked through valleys and stood on mountaintops, always seeking to understand how these ancient stories speak to us today. I'm eager to share this journey with you.

You'll find "Deeper Insight" questions at the end of each chapter. These are designed to encourage you to reflect and engage with the material on a personal level. It's a chance to pause, think deeply, and apply these lessons to your own life. The biblical quotes throughout each chapter were drawn from the NIV version of the Bible on https://www.biblegateway.com/ except for the subchapter stories on Susanna and Judith, which can be found at https://www.kingjamesbibleonline.org/Apocrypha-Books/.

Additionally, both volumes of this book include a list of resources—online forums and study guides—to further your exploration and connect with a community of like-minded individuals. You'll find that journeying with others can offer strength and insight that we often miss when we walk alone.

The lessons in these pages reveal something vital: Your story is still being written. Like these women, your life is part of God's greater plan, no matter how ordinary or complicated it may feel. Your faith, your choices, and your courage have the power to leave a lasting impact on those around you.

As you read, I encourage you to reflect on the strength of these women and the strength God has placed within you. You may identify with Hannah's heartfelt prayers, Mary's quiet trust, or Rizpah's unshakable love. Each of these women reveals a powerful truth: You matter; your faith and your story matter.

As we begin this journey together, I leave you with an inspirational thought: "You are loved beyond measure, and your story matters." May this book inspire you to embrace your own spiritual growth with courage and joy. Let us walk this path together, discovering the strength, wisdom, and love that have been with us all along.

I'm excited to walk this journey with you.

With encouragement and hope,

Hope Maren

P.S. If the stories in this book speak to your heart, I'd be truly grateful if you'd consider leaving an honest review when you finish reading. Your voice can help others discover these faith-building insights and join us on this journey. Thank you for being part of the journey with me.

FOUNDATIONS OF FAITH

1.1 EVE: THE FIRST WOMAN'S LEGACY

Eve's story begins with a celebration of creation, a partnership meant to cultivate and guard the paradise they were given. Imagine being the first woman ever—talk about pressure! Her story isn't just about the infamous apple incident; it's about laying the foundation for humanity and navigating a world of firsts. As women, we face our firsts, whether it's a new job, a move, or simply trying to make it through the day without misplacing our keys.

> *But for Adam no suitable helper was found. So the Lord God caused the man to fall into a deep sleep; and while he was sleeping, he took one of the man's ribs and then closed up the place with flesh. The Lord God made a woman from the rib he had taken out of the man, and he brought her to the man. The man said, "This is now bone of my bones and flesh of my flesh; she shall be called 'woman,' for she was taken out of man.' That is why a man leaves his father and mother and is united*

to his wife, and they become one flesh. Adam and his
wife were both naked and they felt no shame.

— GENESIS 2:20-25 NIV

Eve's role in human history is nothing short of monumental. She wasn't just created from Adam's rib to be a sidekick; she was an equal partner entrusted with the care of the Garden of Eden alongside Adam. The Hebrew word used to describe Eve, "ezer," means ally or helper, highlighting her role as a confidante, not a subordinate. This partnership was about teamwork, not hierarchy, and it's a reminder that our relationships, too, should be built on shared responsibilities and mutual respect.

Then there's the Fall, a story we know all too well. Eve wasn't around when God entrusted the care of the Garden of Eden to Adam, and she wasn't there when God told him not to eat from the Tree of Knowledge.

> *The Lord God took the man and put him in the Garden*
> *of Eden to work it and take care of it. And the Lord*
> *God commanded the man, "you are free to eat from*
> *any tree in the garden; but you must not eat from*
> *the tree of the knowledge of good and evil, for when*
> *you eat from it you will certainly die. The Lord God*
> *said, "It is not good for the man to be alone. I will*
> *make a helper suitable for him."*

— GENESIS 2:15-18 NIV

Eden wasn't just a physical paradise but a place of peace and deep connection with God. The Tree of Knowledge of Good and Evil stood in the garden's center. It was there not as a trap but as a choice between obedience and trust over temptation.

The serpent was persuasive, distorting the truth to plant seeds of doubt and desire in Eve's heart.

> *Now the serpent was more crafty than any of the wild*
> *animals the Lord God had made. He said to the*
> *woman, "Did God really say, you must not eat from*
> *any tree in the garden'?" The woman said to the*
> *serpent, "We may eat fruit from the trees in the*
> *garden, but God did say, 'You must not eat fruit*
> *from the tree that is in the middle of the garden, and*
> *you must not touch it, or you will die.'" "You will*
> *not certainly die," the serpent said to the woman.*
> *"For God knows that when you eat from it your eyes*
> *will be opened, and you will be like God, knowing*
> *good and evil."*

> — GENESIS 3:1-5 NIV

Eve wasn't reckless or rebellious; she was curious, thoughtful, and drawn to understanding and becoming more. The crafty serpent's deception led Eve to eat from the Tree of Knowledge, a decision that changed everything.

Tradition often paints Eve as the one who brought sin into the world, but let's be honest; this narrative oversimplifies her story. It wasn't just a matter of gullibility but a complex choice that speaks to the human desire for wisdom and independence. This choice, however, set the stage for what we call original sin. It teaches us about temptation and the heavy weight of responsibility. Yet, even in her disobedience, there's a glimmer of hope —God's promise of redemption through her offspring. The prophecy in Genesis 3:15 hints at salvation, positioning Eve as a precursor to Mary, whose lineage would eventually lead to Jesus.

This promise of redemption is often called the Protevangelium, or "first gospel".

> *"I will put enmity between you and the woman, and*
> *between your offspring and her offspring; he shall*
> *bruise your head, and you shall bruise his heel."*

— GENESIS 3:15 ESV

Talk about subliminal text! This verse has a surface meaning that can literally be taken as: "If you don't bite me first, I'll be smashing your head in," which is pretty much what happens when we see a snake. The second deeper meaning is more subtle and is considered foundational in Christian theology as it introduces the hope of a savior who will ultimately defeat evil.

Broken down, the key elements of redemption in this verse are as follows:

"Enmity between you and the woman." A division is introduced between humanity and Satan, setting the stage for the conflict between good and evil.

"Between your offspring and her offspring." This line points to a specific lineage, culminating in a direct descendant of Eve who will play a pivotal role in redemption.

"He shall bruise your head." This line foreshadows a mortal blow to Satan, often interpreted as Christ's victory over sin and death.

"You shall bruise his heel." This line acknowledges suffering or harm to the redeemer, as seen in Jesus' crucifixion.

Eve's decisions were profound, shaping her understanding of purpose. Her choice to seek knowledge outside God's guidance reminds us of the delicate balance between companionship and individuality. Her story is a study in contrasts—companionship with Adam and the individuality of making a choice that had far-reaching consequences. It's a reminder that our choices impact not just our lives but the lives of those around us, influencing our purpose and direction.

In reflecting on Eve's narrative, we see ourselves in her shoes. We've all faced moments of temptation and had to deal with the fallout from our decisions. Yet, like Eve, we're offered grace and forgiveness, a chance to find our purpose and realign after life's challenges. Her story encourages us to embrace redemption and growth and to see each mistake as an opportunity for learning and renewal. It's about finding the balance between our roles and our individual paths and recognizing that, despite our flaws, we are part of a greater story of redemption and hope.

Deeper Insight

Consider times in your life when you had to make a difficult choice. Would you make the same choices now? Why or why not? How do you discern truth from lies when faced with temptation? Do your choices reflect trust in God's wisdom over your current understanding of your situation? Why or why not? How does having the ability to choose deepen our connection with God, rather than being forced to obey? In what ways does trusting God's wisdom over our understanding challenge us? How does the story of Eve teach us about finding grace and redemption in our moments of failure? Does her story help you accept God's grace for your mistakes?

Final Thoughts

In the Garden of Eden, Eve lived in perfect harmony with God, Adam, and creation. She was part of a world untouched by sin, where everything was **"very good"** (Genesis 1:31 NIV). However, the serpent influenced her decision to eat the forbidden tree's fruit, changing everything.

Eve's story is about so much more than the fall; it's about humanity, choice, and God's incredible grace. She teaches us to trust God's design, be mindful of temptation, and find hope in His plan for redemption. Eve may have made a mistake, but she also reminds us that our stories don't end with failure. They continue with God's grace.

Eve's story has always struck me as both cautionary and hopeful. I often reflect on the moments in my life where I've faced choices that seemed simple at the time, only to discover their more profound implications later. It's a reminder that our decisions carry weight but also that God's grace is ever-present, ready to restore and renew. Even when I look back on my mistakes, I'm encouraged by the idea that every misstep can be a stepping stone toward greater wisdom and redemption.

I think about the relationships in my life, the people who have supported me through hard times and helped me understand that I am more than my failures. Eve's journey, with all its complexity, teaches me that connection, communication, accountability, and love are vital in navigating life's challenges.

Eve's narrative is a profound exploration of what it means to be human. It's about making choices, facing their consequences, and still finding hope in the promise of redemption. Her story invites us to reflect on our own decisions, seek forgiveness when we falter, and trust that God's plan is more significant than any moment of failure. Let her journey inspire you to embrace your freedom with wisdom, learn from your past, and always hold onto the hope of new beginnings.

Sarai had a comfortable life, living in Ur with her husband Abram when God sent Abram and Sarah out of Ur to live.

> *The Lord made a covenant with Abram and said, "Go*
> *from your country, your people and your father's*
> *household to the land I will show you. I will make*
> *you into a great nation, and I will bless you; I will*
> *make your name great, and you will be a blessing. I*
> *will bless those who bless you, and whoever curses*
> *you I will curse;and all peoples on earth will be*
> *blessed through you."*
>
> — GENESIS 12:1-3 NIV

They found a nice place by the great tree of Moreh and Abram built an altar to the Lord. They didn't stay there long as there was severe famine and Sarai and Abram moved on to stay in Egypt.

Abram was concerned the Egyptians would kill him because he had a beautiful wife, so, as they were coming into Egypt, he asked her to say she was his sister.

> *"I know what a beautiful woman you are. When the*
> *Egyptians see you, they will say, 'This is his wife.'*
> *Then they will kill me but will let you live. Say you*
> *are my sister, so that I will be treated well for your*
> *sake and my life will be spared because of you."*
>
> — GENESIS 12:11-13 NIV

Although this was a questionable arrangement, Abram might've been right to be afraid. Palace officials highly praised Sarai's beauty to the Pharaoh; thus, she was taken into the Pharaoh's palace. It's easy to see why it might be scary to move into a new place as the husband of a beautiful woman. Because of Sarai, Abram was treated well and given gifts of sheep, cattle, donkeys, camels, and servants.

But God was unhappy with this arrangement, as Sarai was supposed to be with Abram. So, the Lord inflicted serious diseases on Pharaoh and his household. Pharaoh confronted Abram and rebuked him for his deception. He ordered them to leave Egypt. Abram and Sarai left, taking the Pharaoh's gifts with them.

Many years later, Abram practiced the same deception. When they moved to Gerar, ruled by King Abimelech, Abram told Sarah to say she was his sister. King Abimelech took Sarah into his household, believing her to be a beautiful, single lady. God intervened by sending Abimelech a dream, telling him not to touch Sarah because she was married.

> "Early the next morning Abimelek summoned all his officials, and when he told them all that had happened, they were very much afraid. Then Abimelek called Abraham in and said, "What have you done to us? How have I wronged you that you have brought such great guilt upon me and my kingdom? You have done things to me that should never be done." And Abimelek asked Abraham, "What was your reason for doing this?" Abraham replied, " I said to myself, 'There is surely no fear of God in this place, and they will kill me because of my wife.' Besides, she really is my sister, the daughter of my father though not of my mother; and she became my wife."
>
> — GENESIS 20:8-13 NIV

Sarah is returned to Abraham, and they are compensated with livestock, silver, and servants. Despite Abraham's shortcomings, God remains faithful, protecting Sarah, thus ensuring His plan for their descendants is fulfilled. Sarah needed to be with Abraham to have the child God had promised her.

> *When Abram was ninety-nine years old, the Lord appeared to him and said, "I am God Almighty, walk before me faithfully and be blameless. This I will make my covenant between me and you and will greatly increase your numbers." Abram fell facedown, and God said to him, "As for me, this is my covenant with you.: You will be the father of many nations. No longer will you be called Abram (Abram means exalted father), your name will be Abraham (Abraham likely means father of many), for I have made you a father of many nations. I will make you very fruitful; I will make nations of you, and kings will come from you. I will establish my covenant as an everlasting covenant between me and you and your descendants after you for the generations to come, to be your God and the God of your descendants after you. The whole land of Canaan, where you now reside as a foreigner, I will give as an everlasting possession to you and your descendants after you; and I will be their God."*

> — GENESIS 17:4-8 NIV

The covenant continues speaking of the covenant of circumcision and then goes on:

> God also said to Abraham, "As for Sarai your wife, you
> are no longer to call her Sarai; her name will be
> Sarah. I will bless her and will surely give you a son
> by her. I will bless her so that she will be the mother
> of nations; kings of peoples will come from her."

— GENESIS 17:15-16 NIV

Abraham was surprised to hear this; after all, he was ninety-nine, and his wife a sweet, young thing of ninety. But he kept these thoughts to himself and did as God asked, making sure all the males in the household were circumcised, himself included.

At about the same time, Sarah was sitting in her tent, doing wifely things, when three strangers came by. She had waited decades for God's promise of a child. At ninety years old, Sarah had just about given up on having children. She was strong, beautiful, and smart but seemed unable to have a baby. She continued to hope; after all, God had told Abram that he'd have descendants as "as numerous as the stars."

Abraham offered the three strangers refreshment and they asked him if Sarah was around.

> "There, in the tent," Abraham said. Then one of them
> said, "I will surely return to you about this time
> next year, and Sarah your wife will have a son."

— GENESIS 18:9-10 NIV

When Sarah hears that she will bear a child, she laughs. Her laughter at this news, as recorded in Genesis 18:12, is not just a chuckle but a complex mixture of disbelief, irony, and perhaps a touch of weariness. Her laugh sounds like years of longing and disappointment confronted by an astonishing promise.

> *Then the Lord said to Abraham, "Why did Sarah laugh and say, 'Will I really have a child, now that I am old?' Is anything too hard for the Lord? I will return to you at the appointed time next year, and Sarah will have a son."*
>
> — GENESIS 18:13-14 NIV

She was Abraham's wife, and he was to become the father of many nations. But it had been many years since she was first promised a child and she was ninety. Ninety! She grew so frustrated and desperate that she even gave her servant Hagar to Abraham to bear a child on her behalf! More on this later, see Chapter 1.3 Hagar: Seeing God in the Wilderness.

However, as we watch her transition from Sarai to Sarah, we see more than a name change. We see a transformation from skepticism to faith, from a woman who laughed at the impossibility to one who would cradle Isaac, the child of promise, in her arms.

Sarah's role in God's covenant is monumental. Her transformation is a testament to the power of faith, even when it seems like an impossibility.

Sarah's story is not just about having a baby in her later years but her fundamental place in fulfilling God's promises to Abraham. The birth of Isaac is more than just a personal victory; it's a fulfillment of a divine promise, a key in the unfolding plan that would lead to a nation. Sarah's influence is woven into the very fabric of the Abrahamic lineage. She is a matriarch in every sense, not just as the mother of Isaac but as a foundational figure in God's grand tapestry of redemption. Her legacy is one of laughter turned to joy and of skepticism turned to faith. She was a living testament to the miraculous power of faith.

Sarah's faith was far from perfect, and that's where her story becomes relatable. She had her moments of doubt and fear, like the time in Egypt when she was taken into Pharaoh's house or when impatience led her to suggest that Abraham have a child with Hagar. These moments of human imperfection are valuable lessons for us. They show that faith does not require perfection but perseverance. Through trials and errors, Sarah's faith grew. She learned to trust in the promises of God, even when the path seemed uncertain. Her story teaches us that as long as we continue to move forward it's okay to stumble along the way.

Sarah lived to the age of 127, and her influence echoes throughout the narrative of God's chosen people, shaping Israel's identity and destiny.

As a matriarch, her legacy is one of strength and resilience. In Jewish tradition, she is a symbol of divine promise and fulfillment. She embodies the hope of a nation and the faithfulness of God's covenant. Her story continues to inspire, reminding us that our lives can have a lasting impact beyond our immediate circumstances.

In today's world, Sarah's faith offers practical insights for facing life's challenges. She encourages us to wait on divine timing and to trust that what seems impossible is often just a stepping stone to something miraculous. Her journey reminds us to embrace faith despite uncertainty, to laugh at the improbable, and to hold on to the promise that God's plans for us are good. Sarah's life reminds us that we can find strength and purpose in the waiting and the doubting, knowing that our faith is part of a larger story.

Deeper Insight

Consider when you have reached out to God, asking for something important or significant. Did you have to wait long before your request was granted? If so, were there times when you wanted to give up? Did you remember that God's timing is frequently different from ours? Did God give you something different from what you asked? How have these prayers shaped your faith? Does faith in God's response encourage you when you feel unworthy or doubtful? What areas of your life could be transformed by believing God makes everything possible?

Final Thoughts

Sarah's story is relatable because it's a vivid reminder that life's delays and detours aren't dead ends; they're part of a larger plan that only God fully understands. There have been times when I've felt stuck in a season of waiting or when my doubts seemed overwhelming. In those moments, remembering Sarah's journey has given me hope. She didn't get everything right from the start, but she became a vital part of God's redemptive plan through her struggles. Her life teaches me that every season, whether filled with promise or pain, has a purpose.

She laughed at God's promises, got frustrated with His timing, and tried to "help" in ways that backfired. Her life is a testament to God's faithfulness and His ability to work through our doubts, struggles, and even our missteps. Her laughter, both of disbelief and joy, reminds us that God's promises will always prevail. He has the power to do things that seem impossible.

Sarah's life is a testament to the beauty of patience, trust, and the transformative power of God's promises. Her journey from uncertainty to the joy of motherhood invites us to believe that God is always working for our good, no matter how long the wait or how deep our doubts. I hope her story inspires you to trust in His timing, embrace your journey with all its ups and downs, and know that every step you take is part of a grand, unfolding narrative of grace.

Picture Hagar, an Egyptian servant, trudging through the wilderness with the sun beating down on her back, her heart heavy with desperation. As a servant, Hagar had little control over her circumstances. Sarah had given her to Abraham in desperation to be a surrogate, to bear a child when it seemed Sarah could not. This was a common but unpopular cultural practice.

> *Now Sarai, Abram's wife, had borne him no children. But she had an Egyptian slave named Hagar; so she said to Abram, "The Lord has kept me from having children. Go, sleep with my slave; perhaps I can build a family through her." Abram agreed to what Sarai said. So after Abram had been living in Canaan ten years, Sarai his wife took her Egyptian slave Hagar and gave her to her husband to be his wife. He slept with Hagar, and she conceived.*
>
> — GENESIS 16:1-4 NIV

She bore Abraham his first son, Ishmael, but fled Sarah and Abraham's household because of Sarah's jealousy of her. In fairness, she wasn't all that crazy about Sarah either. As we delve deeper into Hagar's life, it becomes clear that her struggles are immense. She was a servant, an outsider in Abraham and Sarah's world, caught in a web of power dynamics and personal pain. Her relationship with Sarah was fraught with tension, a reminder of the complex human relationships that resonate with us today.

Hagar's story is one of resilience and blessed with a divine encounter. This tale speaks to the heart of anyone who has ever felt unseen or overlooked. She's in the desert, pregnant and alone, when, in her despair, the angel of the Lord appears to her.

> The angel of the Lord found Hagar near a spring in the desert; it was the spring that is beside the road to Shur. And he said, "Hagar, slave of Sari, where have you come from, and where are you going?" "I'm running away from my mistress Sarai," she answered. Then the angel of the Lord told her, "Go back to your mistress and submit to her." The angel added, "I will increase your descendants so much that they will be too numerous to count." .... "You will give birth to a son. You shall name him Ishmael.."
>
> — GENESIS 16:7-11 NIV

Imagine the shock and relief in Hagar's eyes as she realizes she is not invisible to God. This encounter is not just a divine intervention; it's a revelation. Hagar names God "El Roi," meaning "The God Who Sees Me."

> She gave this name to the Lord who spoke to her: "you are the God who sees me," for she said, "I have now seen the One who sees me."
>
> — GENESIS 16:13 NIV

It's a powerful declaration of faith, a reminder that even in our darkest moments, the Creator sees and knows us. God's promise to Hagar about her son Ishmael's future echoes through the ages, assuring her that he will become a great nation. This promise transforms Hagar's wilderness of despair into a testament of hope and future blessings.

Many are all too familiar with Hagar's challenges as a single mother. She fought to protect and provide for Ishmael in a harsh and unforgiving environment. Her story highlights the courage it takes to endure when the odds are stacked against you.

Hagar was still in Abraham's household when she bore Ishmael, who was circumcised as part of Abraham's covenant. When Sarah finally had her son Isaac, Hagar and Ishmael were still part of Abraham's household. Sarah and Abraham had a big party, a great feast, to celebrate Isaac's being weaned. At that point, Sarah had had enough and told Abraham to cut Hagar and Ishmael loose.

> "Get rid of that slave woman and her son, for that
> woman's son will never share in the inheritance
> with my son Isaac."
>
> — GENESIS 20:10 NIV

This was not one of Sarah's better moments, especially since she had instigated the birth of Hagar's son by Abraham! To Abraham's credit, Sarah's request greatly distressed him. Ishmael was his son, too, after all. God reassured him.

> "Do not be so distressed about the boy and your slave
> woman. Listen to whatever Sarah tells you, because
> it is through Isaac that your offspring wil be
> reckoned. I will make the son of the slave into a
> nation also, because he is your offspring."
>
> — GENESIS 20:11-13 NIV

So Abraham gave Hagar some food and water the morning of the following day and sent her off. Now, Hagar is in the desert with a small child and only the food and water she can carry. Can you imagine her desperation, her fear? She was thinking to herself, "I can't watch my son die!" She was probably having a panic attack when God said to her,

> "What is the matter, Hagar? Do not be afraid; God has heard the boy crying as he lies there. Lift the boy up and take him by the hand, for I will make him into a great nation. Then God opened her eyes and she saw a well of water. So she went and filled the skin with water and gave the boy a drink. God was with the boy as he grew up. He lived in the desert and became an archer.

— GENESIS 20:17-20 NIV

Hagar's journey was not just about survival; it was about finding strength in the face of adversity, about rising above her circumstances with dignity and resolve.

Hagar's legacy is one of unyielding perseverance. She raised her son in the wilderness, a testament to her unbreakable spirit. Despite the hardships, she remained resilient, embodying the strength that would lead her son to fulfill God's promise as a father of nations. Hagar's role in God's plan for Ishmael is a powerful reminder that even those on the fringes, whom society often overlooks, are integral to God's grand design. Her story is a beacon of hope for all who find themselves in the wilderness, navigating life's challenges with faith and determination.

In today's world, Hagar's experience resonates with those who feel marginalized or unseen. Her story offers insights into God's unwavering faithfulness to the marginalized, encouraging anyone who feels abandoned or invisible. In a society that often overlooks the worth of individuals based on status or circumstance, Hagar's narrative reminds us of the importance of acknowledging personal worth and dignity.

Her experiences teach us about resilience, not as a mere survival tactic but as a profound act of faith. By embracing Hagar's story, we learn to develop strength through faith, to trust in a God who sees us, and his love knows no boundaries, even when we feel lost in the wilderness.

Deeper Insight

Think about a time when you felt small or unimportant. Were you encouraged by knowing that God sees you, always, and that He notices your pain? What does Hagar teach us about trusting God in desperate situations? How does her story challenge us to examine how we treat those who are vulnerable or dependent on us? What can we do to reflect God's compassion and kindness in situations where we have influence over others?

Final Thoughts

Hagar's narrative speaks to the deep, often unspoken part of our hearts that feels overlooked or undervalued. I find comfort in knowing that God doesn't turn a blind eye to our struggles. He meets us in our most desperate moments, offering hope and promising a future we might never have dared to imagine. Her story challenges me to be more aware of the people around me who might be suffering in silence and to remember that even the smallest, most seemingly insignificant life is precious in God's eyes.

Hagar's story reminds us that God's love knows no boundaries. He is the God who sees, hears, and provides for us, even when the world has cast us aside. Her journey shows that God forgets no one, and her faith and resilience continue to inspire us today.

Hagar's life also reminds us that our circumstances do not define our worth. Despite hardships and the labels imposed by society, God values and has a plan for each of us. Her journey from despair to the promise of a great future is a powerful testimony of God's enduring love and care. I hope her story inspires you to trust in God's promises, seek hope in your darkest moments, and remember you, too, are seen, valued, and deeply loved by Him.

Rebekah's story begins when she leaves her family on a journey to marry Isaac. Think of her courage to travel to a distant land, leaving everything familiar behind. She was from the family of Nahor, Abraham's brother, and lived in Mesopotamia. When Abraham's servant arrived seeking a wife for Isaac, Abraham's son, her life changed dramatically. She met him at the well, showing kindness and hospitality by offering him and his camels water. This act of generosity led the servant to recognize her as the woman God had chosen for Isaac.

> *"When I came to the spring today, I said, 'Lord, God of my master Abraham, if you will, please grant success to the journey on which I have come. See, I am standing beside this spring. If a young woman comes out to draw water and I say to her, "Please let me drink a little water from your jar," and if she says to me, "Drink, and I'll draw water for your camels too," let her be the one the Lord has chosen for my master's son.'*
>
> *"Before I finished praying in my heart, Rebekah came out, with her jar on her shoulder. She went down to the spring and drew water, and I said to her, 'Please give me a drink.'*
>
> *"She quickly lowered her jar from her shoulder and said, 'Drink, and I'll water your camels too.' So I drank, and she watered the camels also.*
>
> *"I asked her, 'Whose daughter are you?'*
>
> *"She said, 'The daughter of Bethuel son of Nahor, whom Milkah bore to him.'*
>
> *"Then I put the ring in her nose and the bracelets on her arms, and I bowed down and worshiped the Lord. I praised the Lord, the God of my master Abraham,*

who had led me on the right road to get the grand-
daughter of my master's brother for his son.

— GENESIS 24:42-48 NIV

Her decision wasn't just about marrying Isaac but about stepping into a pivotal role in God's unfolding promise. Later, as a
mother, Rebekah plays a crucial role in shaping the destiny of
her sons, helping Jacob secure Isaac's blessing, which was
intended for Esau. Rebekah's actions set in motion events that
would shape the fate of nations.

After years of barrenness, she became pregnant with twins.
During her pregnancy, she felt great turmoil within her and
reached out to God for guidance. God told her that her sons,
Jacob and Esau, would become two nations and that the older
would serve the younger, a revelation that must have seemed as
strange as it was profound. This prophecy placed Rebekah at
the heart of God's plan, positioning her as a key player in
continuing the covenant with Abraham.

> *Isaac prayed to the Lord on behalf of his wife, because*
> *she was childless. The Lord answered his prayer,*
> *and his wife Rebekah became pregnant. The babies*
> *jostled each other within her, and she said, "Why is*
> *this happening to me?" So she went to inquire of the*
> *Lord.*
> *The Lord said to her,*
> *"Two nations are in your womb,*
> *and two peoples from within you will be separated;*
> *one people will be stronger than the other,*
> *and the older will serve the younger."*
>
> *When the time came for her to give birth, there were*
> *twin boys in her womb. The first to come out was*

red, and his whole body was like a hairy garment;
so they named him Esau. After this, his brother
came out, with his hand grasping Esau's heel; so he
was named Jacob. Isaac was sixty years old when
Rebekah gave birth to them.

— GENESIS 25:21-26 NIV

Now, let's talk about trust and deception, which makes Rebekah's story particularly intriguing. We find her in a tricky situation where she has to balance her faith in God with a cunning plan to ensure Jacob receives Isaac's blessing. She favored Jacob over Esau and orchestrated a plan for Jacob to deceive Isaac and receive the blessing intended for Esau. Jacob was named for his birth grasping Esau's heel, but it also can mean someone who takes advantage or deceives.

Time went on and the boys grew. Esau had a very casual attitude about his birthright. On one occasion, he casually gave his birthright in exchange for stew. This flippant action was a foreshadowing of what was to come.

When Isaac was very old and nearly blind, he asked for his eldest son, Esau, to come to him.

Isaac said, "I am now an old man and don't know the
day of my death. Now then, get your equipment—
your quiver and bow—and go out to the open
country to hunt some wild game for me. Prepare me
the kind of tasty food I like and bring it to me to eat,
so that I may give you my blessing before I die."

— GENESIS 27:2-4 NIV

Rebekah overheard this and called Jacob to bring two young goats to her so that she could prepare them as Isaac liked. She told him to dress as Esau and take the food to Isaac so he would receive the blessing intended for Esau.

> *So he went and got them and brought them to his mother, and she prepared some tasty food, just the way his father liked it. Then Rebekah took the best clothes of Esau her older son, which she had in the house, and put them on her younger son Jacob. She also covered his hands and the smooth part of his neck with the goatskins. Then she handed to her son Jacob the tasty food and the bread she had made.*
> *"Yes, my son," he answered. "Who is it?"*
>
> — GENESIS 27:14-18 NIV

Isaac was uncertain which of his sons had brought the food. The voice was Jacob's, but his scent and skin were that of Esau. Even so, Isaac was convinced, so Isaac blessed him, and very shortly afterward, Esau came in with tasty food. It was then they discovered Jacob's deception. The blessing meant Jacob received his father's worldly goods. Isaac, believing he was blessing his firstborn, gave Jacob the blessing of prosperity and dominion. Esau's anger was so intense that Jacob had to flee for his life.

> *His father Isaac asked him, "Who are you?" "I am your son," he answered, "your firstborn, Esau." Isaac trembled violently and said, "Who was it, then, that hunted game and brought it to me? I ate it just before you came and I blessed him—and indeed he will be blessed!"*
> *When Esau heard his father's words, he burst out with a loud and bitter cry and said to his father, "Bless me*

—me too, my father!" But he said, "Your brother came deceitfully and took your blessing." Esau said, "Isn't he rightly named Jacob? This is the second time he has taken advantage of me: He took my birthright, and now he's taken my blessing!" Then he asked, "Haven't you reserved any blessing for me?"

Isaac answered Esau, "I have made him lord over you and have made all his relatives his servants, and I have sustained him with grain and new wine. So what can I possibly do for you, my son?"

Esau said to his father, "Do you have only one blessing, my father? Bless me too, my father!" Then Esau wept aloud.

His father Isaac answered him,
"Your dwelling will be away from the earth's richness, away from the dew of heaven above.
You will live by the sword and you will serve your brother.
But when you grow restless, you will throw his yoke from off your neck."

— GENESIS 27:32-40 NIV

Rebekah's decision to deceive Isaac was driven by her trust in God's word about her sons, yet her methods were less straightforward. It's a reminder that sometimes, even with the best intentions, our actions can lead us into murky moral waters. Perhaps you've found yourself in a similar spot, caught between trusting divine guidance and the messy reality of human choices. Rebekah teaches us that life isn't always black and white; it's often a shade of gray, requiring faith and wisdom.

In time Jacob and Esau reconciled. Jacob worked under his uncle Laban for years, married Leah and Rachel, and had children. These experiences humbled Jacob, preparing him for eventual reconciliation. Years later, Jacob and Esau met again. Fearing Esau's wrath, Jacob sent gifts ahead and approached him humbly. Esau surprised him by embracing him warmly. Their reconciliation is a beautiful moment of grace, forgiveness, and healing. More about their reconciliation can be found in Genesis 33.

Rebekah's influence didn't stop with Jacob's blessing. Her favoring of Jacob over Esau set off a chain of events that would have long-lasting repercussions on their family dynamics. While fulfilling God's prophecy, her actions brought conflict and division to her family and came at a cost. Jacob was forced to flee, and she likely never saw him again.

As many of us know from our families, favoritism can be a double-edged sword. It might be as subtle as who gets the biggest slice of pie at Thanksgiving or as significant as determining a family's future. In Rebekah's case, her actions led to a sibling rivalry that echoed through generations. It's a poignant reminder of how our choices as parents or mentors can shape the destinies of those we love. Her story challenges us to consider the weight of our influence—how it can nurture or fracture relationships.

So, what can we learn from Rebekah today? Her story encourages us to make decisions with integrity and faith, acknowledging her narrative's strengths and weaknesses. We're reminded to trust in divine guidance, even when the path ahead is complex. You may face a decision that feels like a chess game, requiring strategy and foresight. Rebekah's life invites us to reflect on how we navigate these moments, balancing cunning with a sincere heart. Remember, it's okay not to have all the answers. What matters is the trust we place in God's promises and the courage to act upon them with grace and wisdom.

Deeper Insight

Reflect on a time when you benefitted or were the victim of favoritism. How did you respond? What can we learn from conflict that might arise from favoritism? How can we navigate the challenges of partiality or bias in our relationships? How can we discern the difference between trusting God's timing and taking control of a situation? Have you ever acted out of impatience or fear? How did God work through your choices? What situations in your life would benefit from intentionally seeking God's guidance? How might God call you to use your strengths and influence for His purposes despite your imperfections? Does Rebekah's story encourage you to consider your relationships and any biases that might impact those around you?

Final Thoughts

Rebekah's story makes me think of times when I've had to take a leap of faith without knowing the outcome. Sometimes, I would say yes, I am exactly where I'm supposed to be, doing what I'm supposed to be doing. Other times, I've hesitated and wondered if I have the courage to act and trust God's plan. Rebekah's imperfections remind me that God works through flawed people—like me and you. Knowing that we don't have to be perfect for God to use us is comforting.

Let's not forget the family drama. Every family has its quirks, but Rebekah's favoritism and the fallout between Jacob and Esau make me wonder how often I let my biases affect my relationships. It's a gentle nudge to be mindful of how my actions shape those around me. Rebekah's story encourages us to trust God in the big decisions, to act with kindness in the small ones, and to seek wisdom as we navigate the complex relationships that define our lives.

Zipporah was one of the seven daughters of Jethro (also known as Reuel), a Midianite priest. She met Moses at a well, a common place for key biblical encounters. Moses defended Zipporah and her sisters from shepherds who tried to drive them away. This act of bravery led Jethro to invite Moses into his home, and soon after, Moses married Zipporah. Together, they had two sons, Gershom and Eliezer. Zipporah likely stabilized Moses' life; their lives together were humble and quiet compared to his former life in Pharoah's palace.

Moses, the man tasked by God with leading the Israelites out of Egypt, is suddenly struck with a life-threatening illness. It's a crisis moment that could derail the entire plan of deliverance. The cause of Moses' illness is often thought to be Moses' failure to circumcise his son, a critical sign of the covenant between God and His people.

His wife, Zipporah, finds herself in a situation that demands immediate action. Without hesitation, she performs the circumcision of their son.

> At a lodging place on the way, the Lord met Moses and
> was about to kill him. But Zipporah took a flint
> knife, cut off her son's foreskin and touched Moses'
> feet with it. "Surely you are a bridegroom of blood to
> me," she said. So the Lord let him alone.

> — EXODUS 4:24-26 NIV

This decisive act saved Moses. Her quick thinking and spiritual insight are remarkable. She recognizes the spiritual significance of this act, understanding that it's a covenantal sign essential for Moses to fulfill his God-given mission. In doing so, she steps into a role that preserves not just her husband's life but the future of an entire nation.

Zipporah's intervention is a testament to the power of intuition and the ability to act decisively under pressure. Her understanding of the spiritual implications of the situation speaks volumes about her faith and wisdom. In a moment of crisis, she doesn't falter. Instead, she takes a bold step, demonstrating that faith is not just about belief but about action. Her story invites us to consider how to trust our intuition and spiritual insight when faced with critical moments. It teaches us that sometimes, the most profound acts of faith are the ones that require immediate and courageous decisions, even when the path ahead seems unclear.

The implications of Zipporah's actions ripple through her family and beyond. By performing the circumcision, she reaffirms her family's commitment to God's covenant, strengthening their collective faith and mission. Her intervention ensures that Moses can continue his God-ordained task of leading the Israelites to freedom. This act of faith preserves Moses' mission and fortifies their family's bond to God's promises. It's a powerful reminder that our actions have the potential to uphold and advance our commitments to what is sacred and purposeful.

Zipporah's story reveals her as a woman of action and courage. She stepped into a dangerous and uncomfortable situation to protect her family and align with God's covenant. Her life wasn't easy—married to a man called to a monumental mission, she likely faced challenges in understanding and supporting his divine calling. Yet she remained a critical part of Moses' story, providing stability and courage in moments of crisis.

In our lives today, Zipporah's example challenges us to act decisively in faith-driven situations. Whether making a difficult decision at work, navigating family challenges, or stepping out into community service, we're called to trust our intuition and spiritual insight. These moments often come without warning, demanding quick thinking and unwavering trust in God's guidance. Zipporah's story encourages us to embrace these opportunities and act boldly and with conviction, knowing that our faith-driven actions can impact our lives and the lives of those around us.

As we reflect on Zipporah's courage and insight, let us find inspiration in her legacy of faith and action. Her story is a powerful reminder that even in the most unexpected circumstances, we are equipped to make decisions that honor our commitments and advance our divine purpose. In doing so, we strengthen our relationship with God and affirm our place in the unfolding story of His promise to the world. Let's carry this wisdom forward, allowing it to guide us daily as we strive to live with faith, courage, and purpose.

Deeper Insight

Was there ever a time when you needed to take immediate action or make a sudden choice for which you were unprepared? How did you respond, and would you do anything differently today? How can we navigate faith and cultural identity when they intersect or challenge each other? What areas of your life might God be calling you to deeper obedience or action, even if it feels uncomfortable? How can we draw strength from Zipporah's example when we feel overlooked or unsure of our impact? What does Zipporah's story teach us about the importance of courage and faith, even when our contributions might go unnoticed by others?

Final Thoughts

I'm inspired by stories like Zipporah's, where the details may be sparse, but the impact is profound. There have been times when I've had to make quick decisions without knowing all the answers, and I remember wondering if I had the courage to act in the moment. Zipporah's story challenges me to trust that God can work through even the most unexpected actions. It reminds me that every small, faithful step, every act of support, and every moment of courage contributes to God's bigger plan.

Zipporah's story is one of quiet strength and decisive faith. She reminds us that God often calls us to act in ways that may seem small but have profound importance. Her courage and obedience continue to inspire us, showing us that faith in action can shape history, even in the most unexpected ways. Zipporah reminds us that even those who appear briefly in Scripture can teach us profound lessons. Her story speaks to the complexities of faith, the importance of obedience, and the courage it takes to act in critical moments.

Zipporah's life, though only briefly mentioned in the Bible, teaches us that our roles in God's story are significant, no matter how small they may seem. Her courage, practical wisdom, and willingness to act when it mattered most remind us that faith is not always loud or dramatic—it can be found in the quiet, decisive actions of those who trust God with their whole hearts. I hope her story inspires you to step forward in faith, support those around you, and embrace the often mysterious ways God works through us all.

Reflections on Foundations of Faith

As I close this chapter on Foundations of Faith, I think of the examples given to me by the stories of these women; Eve's choice, Sarah's laugh, Hagar's banishment, Rebekah's favoritism, and Zipporah's decisive act. These women were just like us,

making decisions and choices based on the available information. We can see how faith plays a fundamental part in the
outcome of their choices. We are reminded that faith is not
about perfection but about persistent trust in the One who is
always faithful. Let us be inspired to live boldly, love deeply, and
walk confidently, believing God is always with us and working
for our good.

COURAGE AND LEADERSHIP

2.1 SHIPHRAH AND PUAH: DEFYING INJUSTICE

Shiphrah and Puah were midwives who helped deliver Hebrew babies during Israel's time of slavery in Egypt. Imagine these two women working diligently in ancient Egypt's hot, dusty rooms. Pharaoh commanded them to end the lives of every male Hebrew child at birth.

Shiphrah and Puah feared God and refused to obey Pharaoh. However, they had something more potent than fear: faith and a mighty dose of moral courage. They disobeyed Pharaoh, spared the babies, and lied when questioned.

> The king of Egypt said to the Hebrew midwives, whose names were Shiphrah and Puah, "When you are helping the Hebrew women during childbirth on the delivery stool, if you see that the baby is a boy, kill him; but if it is a girl, let her live." The midwives, however, feared God and did not do what the king of Egypt had told them to do; they let the boys live. Then the king of Egypt summoned the midwives

and asked them, "Why have you done this? Why
have you let the boys live?"
The midwives answered Pharaoh, "Hebrew women are
not like Egyptian women; they are vigorous and
give birth before the midwives arrive."

— EXODUS 1:15-19 NIV

Shiphrah and Puah's decision to defy Pharaoh's orders wasn't just an act of civil disobedience—it was an act of profound integrity. They risked their own lives to preserve life because they feared and revered God more than any earthly king.

Their refusal to comply with Pharaoh's command is a testament to their unwavering moral compass.

What they did was nothing less than revolutionary. These women stood firm in a society where the king's word was absolute. They employed a bit of strategic deception, telling Pharaoh that Hebrew women were too vigorous and gave birth before the midwives could arrive. This act of defiance was not just a refusal to do wrong but a powerful statement against injustice. It's akin to the modern-day whistleblower who stands up against corruption at significant personal risk.

The impact of their courage is immeasurable. Thanks to these two women, a generation of Hebrew boys survived, including one particularly important baby named Moses. Their actions directly contributed to the survival of Moses, the future deliverer of Israel, and laid a foundation for God's plan to liberate His people. Their bravery allowed the Hebrew population to grow and thrive, laying the groundwork for the eventual Exodus.

Shiphrah and Puah preserved hope and promise for their people by preserving life. Because of their faithfulness, God blessed

Shiphrah and Puah with families of their own. Their bravery played a vital role in preserving the Israelite nation, demonstrating how God works through those who trust Him. It's a powerful reminder of how individual acts of courage can ripple out to affect entire communities, even nations. Shiphrah and Puah teach us that sometimes, standing up for what is right means standing up against what is wrong, even when it comes from the top.

In today's world, their story challenges us to examine the systems of injustice we encounter. Whether in the workplace, our communities, or broader societal structures, we are called to act with integrity and courage. This means standing firm in our convictions, advocating for those who cannot speak for themselves, and challenging unjust systems with the weapons of truth and love. Like Shiphrah and Puah, we must find the strength to resist oppression and champion the dignity of every human life.

Deeper Insight

Has there ever been a time when you faced a decision that impacted your morals, your faith, or your values? How did you respond, and what guided your decision? Reflect on the courage of Shiphrah and Puah and think about how their actions might inspire you to act in future situations where integrity is at stake. How might their example inspire us to advocate for the marginalized and powerless in our communities? How can we cultivate the kind of faith that enables us to stand firm in the face of opposition? How does your reverence for God influence your decisions? Does their story inspire you to make courageous choices in difficult situations?

Final Thoughts

Shiphrah and Puah's story is about doing the right thing, even when it's terrifying. Their refusal to comply with Pharaoh's orders may have seemed like a small act, but it preserved an entire generation. Never underestimate the power of standing up for what's right. Courage isn't always loud or dramatic; sometimes, it's as quiet as saying, *"No, I won't do this wrong thing,"* even when it's costly.

It also challenges me to think about times when I've faced pressure to compromise. Am I willing to stand firm, even when no one else sees the cost of my decision? Their story is a powerful reminder that standing up for what's right can change the world in ways we may never see. They were ordinary women, but their extraordinary faith and courage made them heroes in God's plan. Their example challenges us to trust God, act boldly, and protect those who cannot protect themselves.

2.2 MIRIAM: LEADING THROUGH SONG AND FAITH

In the dusty streets of Egypt under the relentless sun, a young girl named Miriam grew up amidst the cries of her enslaved people. Her early years were spent witnessing the harsh realities of life under Pharaoh's rule, yet she carried the spark of hope within her.

Her journey begins in Exodus 2, where she watches over her baby brother Moses as a young girl with a protective love beyond her years. It was during the period when Pharaoh ordered all Hebrew baby boys to be killed. When Pharaoh's daughter discovers Moses in the basket on the Nile River and decides to keep him, Miriam bravely approaches her. She offers to find a Hebrew woman to nurse him. This quick and brave act ingeniously reunites Moses with his mother.

> But when she could hide him no longer, she got a
> papyrus basket for him and coated it with tar and
> pitch. Then she placed the child in it and put it
> among the reeds along the bank of the Nile. His
> sister stood at a distance to see what would happen
> to him.
> Then Pharaoh's daughter went down to the Nile to
> bathe, and her attendants were walking along the
> riverbank. She saw the basket among the reeds and
> sent her female slave to get it. She opened it and saw
> the baby. He was crying, and she felt sorry for him.
> "This is one of the Hebrew babies," she said.
> Then his sister asked Pharaoh's daughter, "Shall I go
> and get one of the Hebrew women to nurse the baby
> for you?" "Yes, go," she answered. So the girl went
> and got the baby's mother. Pharaoh's daughter said
> to her, "Take this baby and nurse him for me, and I

will pay you." So the woman took the baby and
nursed him.

— EXODUS 2:3-9 NIV

As Miriam grew older, she watched God's miracles unfold, from
the plagues that shook Egypt to the night of the first Passover.
Each event was a testament to divine power, a glimmer of
freedom on the horizon. Her journey from captivity to liberation wasn't just physical; it was a spiritual awakening that
defined her role in the history of Israel.

Miriam's leadership during the Exodus was nothing short of
extraordinary. As the Israelites crossed the Red Sea with the
waters parting miraculously, leaving their chains behind,
Miriam led the women in a song of triumph. Picture her,
tambourine in hand, leading a chorus of spirited voices to celebrate their newfound freedom.

This wasn't just a moment of joy but a declaration of faith, a
communal acknowledgment of God's deliverance. As a prophetess, Miriam held a position of authority and respect alongside
her brothers, Moses and Aaron. Her leadership was integral to
the fabric of Israel's identity, offering strength and guidance in a
time of uncertainty. In song and counsel, Miriam's voice echoed
through the camp as a testament to the power of faith and the
promise of freedom.

The significance of Miriam's song, often referred to as the Song
of the Sea, cannot be overstated. This ancient hymn, found in
Exodus 15:20-21, is one of the earliest examples of Hebrew
poetry, celebrating not only a military victory but a spiritual
one. Through her song, Miriam united the people in a shared
expression of gratitude and faith. Music and poetry have always
been powerful tools for leadership, capable of inspiring and
uniting communities.

Miriam's Song or Song of the Sea (Exodus 15:20-21 NIV)

> *Then Miriam the prophet, Aaron's sister, took a timbrel*
> *in her hand, and all the women followed her, with*
> *timbrels and dancing.*
> *Miriam sang to them:*
> *"Sing to the Lord,*
> *for he is highly exalted.*
> *Both horse and driver*
> *he has hurled into the sea."*
>
> — EXODUS 15:20-21 NIV

Miriam's song was more than a melody; it was a rallying cry reinforcing the Israelites' collective identity and faith in God's promises. It showed that leadership could be as much about inspiring the heart as guiding the hand.

Yet, Miriam's path was not without its challenges. Even leaders face moments of weakness and dissent. In Numbers 12, we read about Miriam speaking against Moses, questioning his unique relationship with God.

> *Miriam and Aaron began to talk against Moses because*
> *of his Cushite wife, for he had married a Cushite.*
> *"Has the Lord spoken only through Moses?" they*
> *asked. "Hasn't he also spoken through us?" and the*
> *Lord heard this.*
>
> — NUMBERS 12:1-2 NIV

This act of defiance brought consequences; Miriam was struck with leprosy and temporarily set outside the camp. It was a humbling experience, a reminder of the importance of unity and respect within leadership. Her eventual restoration speaks to the power of forgiveness and the value of learning from our mistakes.

> *The anger of the Lord burned against them, and he left*
> *them. When the cloud lifted from above the tent,*
> *Miriam's skin was leprous—it became as white as*
> *snow. Aaron turned toward her and saw that she*
> *had a defiling skin disease, and he said to Moses,*
> *"Please, my lord, I ask you not to hold against us the*
> *sin we have so foolishly committed. Do not let her be*
> *like a stillborn infant coming from its mother's*
> *womb with its flesh half eaten away."*
> *So Moses cried out to the Lord, "Please, God, heal her!"*
> *The Lord replied to Moses, "If her father had spit in*
> *her face, would she not have been in disgrace for*
> *seven days? Confine her outside the camp for seven*
> *days; after that she can be brought back." So*
> *Miriam was confined outside the camp for seven*
> *days, and the people did not move on till she was*
> *brought back.*

> — NUMBERS 12:9-15 NIV

Miriam's story teaches us about humility and the need to balance personal opinions with the collective good. Leadership isn't just about leading boldly; it's about knowing when to listen when to step back, and when to seek reconciliation. Even the most faithful leaders can stumble.

Miriam's legacy of faith and leadership endures as a beacon of inspiration. Her influence on the Israelite women was profound, encouraging them to find their voices and claim their roles in the community. Miriam's emotional and spiritual impact resonated long after her passing, recorded in Numbers 20, commemorated in Jewish tradition, and celebrated in rituals like Miriam's Cup at the Passover Seder. Her importance is underscored in Micah 6:4, where God lists her alongside Moses and Aaron as key leaders who delivered Israel from Egypt. Her role as a leader and prophetess was recognized for generations.

> *I brought you up out of Egypt and redeemed you from*
> *the land of slavery.*
> *I sent Moses to lead you, also Aaron and Miriam.*

— MICAH 6:4 NIV

Her life exemplifies the power of women in spiritual and community leadership, offering a model of strength, creativity, and resilience. Today, Miriam's example inspires us to embrace leadership roles, to lead with authenticity and vision, and to use our voices to inspire and uplift others. Whether through song, word, or deed, we are reminded that leadership is an art of expression, a dance of faith and courage.

Deeper Insight

Consider how your family relationships shape your choices. How might you support and encourage your family in their choices? Do you practice open communication with your family and loved ones? How might you extend compassion and understanding in a difficult situation? Do you react with jealousy or gratitude when others seem to have more recognition or blessings? How does her restoration teach us about God's mercy, even when we fall short? How can we use worship and celebration to encourage and unite others in our families and faith communities? How often do you take time to celebrate answered prayers or blessings in your life?

Final Thoughts

I think about Miriam's journey because it's so human—filled with moments of brilliant faith and times of real struggle. There have been occasions when I've felt strong and capable, only to be humbled by my own shortcomings. Miriam's story reminds me that our failures do not define us; they're opportunities for growth, learning, and deeper reliance on God's grace. Although she experienced a humbling mistake, she was still recognized as a leader in her community. Her courage inspires me to embrace my life's victories and lessons.

Miriam wasn't afraid to act when her family needed her, and her role as a leader and prophetess remained a part of her legacy. Although a strong, courageous leader she was not infallible. Her criticism of Moses shows how pride and jealousy can creep into even the most faithful hearts. Her story reminds us to guard against these feelings and trust God's plan for others, even when it looks different from our own.

In her triumphs and struggles, we see a reflection of our own journey of faith. Miriam's life is a testament to the fact that authentic leadership involves both celebrating God's deliverance and being open to learning from our missteps. Her story encourages us to care for others, worship with a humble and thankful heart, and seek forgiveness when needed. I hope her journey inspires you to recognize that every part of your story —your triumphs, struggles, and moments of humility—is woven into God's larger tapestry of grace and redemption.

2.3 DEBORAH: WISDOM AND WARFARE

Imagine a time when leadership was a men's club, with the sign "no girls allowed" prominently displayed. Now, picture Deborah: a woman who walked into that club and took charge of it while balancing wisdom and warfare. Deborah, Judges 4-5, held a dual role as a judge and prophetess in ancient Israel, a combination as rare as finding a unicorn in your backyard.

Judges in those days weren't just sitting around in robes making gavel noises; they were the arbiters of justice and leaders in times of crisis. Deborah administered justice under the famous palm tree synonymous with her leadership, which was literally called the Palm of Deborah.

Her role as a prophetess gave her spiritual authority, allowing her to guide the people with divine insight. In a society where women were often relegated to the background, Deborah stood as a beacon of leadership, her voice respected and her decisions trusted. Her standing in her community wasn't just a feat; it was a revolution in a patriarchal context, challenging the norms and redefining the image of leadership.

On the battlefield, Deborah's strategic guidance was crucial in leading Israel to victory against the Canaanites, particularly the formidable Sisera. She sent for Barak and had him come to her to discuss his battle strategy and deliver a prophecy of victory.

She sent for Barak son of Abinoam from Kedesh in
Naphtali and said to him, "The Lord, the God of
Israel, commands you: 'Go, take with you ten thou-
sand men of Naphtali and Zebulun and lead them
up to Mount Tabor. I will lead Sisera, the
commander of Jabin's army, with his chariots and
his troops to the Kishon River and give him into
your hands..'"

— JUDGES 4:6-7 NIV

He was hesitant and wouldn't go unless she went with him. She told Barak the credit for the victory would go to a woman if she went with him. He was okay with that, so Deborah went with him. As it turns out, another woman was responsible for delivering Sisera; you can learn more about that in the section that discusses Jael.

When Sisera learned that Barak and his army had gone up Mount Tabor, Sisera took his army and followed.

Then Deborah said to Barak, "Go! This is the day the
Lord has given Sisera into your hands. Has not the
Lord gone ahead of you?" So Barak went down
Mount Tabor, with ten thousand men following
him. At Barak's advance, the Lord routed Sisera and
all his chariots and army by the sword, and Sisera
got down from his chariot and fled on foot.

— JUDGES 4:14-15 NIV

Her confidence wasn't just a motivational facade but grounded in divine assurance. With her guidance, the Israelites executed a surprise attack that rendered Sisera's chariots useless, proving that brains often beat brawn. Deborah and Barak had devised a battle plan to outsmart the enemy. After Israel's victory, Deborah sang a song of praise with Barak. The Song of Deborah, found in Judges 5, is a poetic retelling of this triumph, celebrating the courage and faith that led to victory.

The Song of Deborah (Judges 5:1-31 NIV)

On that day Deborah and Barak son of Abinoam sang
*   this song:*
"When the princes in Israel take the lead, when the
*   people willingly offer themselves—praise the Lord!*

Hear this, you kings! Listen, you rulers!
I, even I, will sing to the Lord; I will praise the Lord, the
*   God of Israel, in song.*
"When you, Lord, went out from Seir, when you
*   marched from the land of Edom, the earth shook,*
*   the heavens poured, the clouds poured down water.*
The mountains quaked before the Lord, the One of
*   Sinai, before the Lord, the God of Israel.*

In the days of Shamgar son of Anath, in the days of
*   Jael, the highways were abandoned; travelers took to*
*   winding paths.*
Villagers in Israel would not fight; they held back until
*   I, Deborah, arose, until I arose, a mother in Israel.*
God chose new leaders when war came to the city gates,
*   but not a shield or spear was seen among forty*
*   thousand in Israel.*
My heart is with Israel's princes, with the willing
*   volunteers among the people.*
Praise the Lord!

You who ride on white donkeys, sitting on your saddle

blankets, and you who walk along the road,
consider the voice of the singers at the watering
places.
They recite the victories of the Lord, the victories of his
villagers in Israel.
Then the people of the Lord went down to the city gates.
'Wake up, wake up, Deborah!
Wake up, wake up, break out in song!
Arise, Barak!
Take captive your captives, son of Abinoam.'

The remnant of the nobles came down; the people of the
Lord came down to me against the mighty.
Some came from Ephraim, whose roots were in Amalek;
Benjamin was with the people who followed you.
From Makir captains came down, from Zebulun those
who bear a commander's staff.

The princes of Issachar were with Deborah; yes,
Issachar was with Barak, sent under his command
into the valley.
In the districts of Reuben there was much searching of
heart.
Why did you stay among the sheep pens to hear the
whistling for the flocks?
In the districts of Reuben there was much searching of
heart.
Gilead stayed beyond the Jordan.
And Dan, why did he linger by the ships?

Asher remained on the coast and stayed in his coves.
The people of Zebulun risked their very lives; so did
Naphtali on the terraced fields.
Kings came, they fought, the kings of Canaan fought.

At Taanach, by the waters of Megiddo, they took no
    plunder of silver.
From the heavens the stars fought, from their courses
    they fought against Sisera.
The river Kishon swept them away, the age-old river,
    the river Kishon.

March on, my soul; be strong!
Then thundered the horses' hooves—galloping,
    galloping go his mighty steeds.
'Curse Meroz,' said the angel of the Lord.
'Curse its people bitterly, because they did not come to
    help the Lord, to help the Lord against the mighty.'

Most blessed of women be Jael, the wife of Heber the
    Kenite, most blessed of tent-dwelling women.
He asked for water, and she gave him milk; in a bowl fit
    for nobles she brought him curdled milk.
Her hand reached for the tent peg, her right hand for
    the workman's hammer.
She struck Sisera, she crushed his head, she shattered
    and pierced his temple.
At her feet he sank, he fell; there he lay.
At her feet he sank, he fell; where he sank, there he fell
    —dead.

Through the window peered Sisera's mother; behind the
    lattice she cried out,
'Why is his chariot so long in coming?
Why is the clatter of his chariots delayed?'
The wisest of her ladies answer her; indeed, she keeps
    saying to herself,
'Are they not finding and dividing the spoils:
a woman or two for each man, colorful garments as

plunder for Sisera, colorful garments embroidered,
highly embroidered garments for my neck—all this
as plunder?'

So may all your enemies perish, Lord!
But may all who love you be like the sun when it rises
in its strength."

Then the land had peace forty years.

— JUDGES 5:1-31 NIV

Deborah's ability to combine wisdom with action exemplifies what it means to lead from the front, with faith as your shield and strategy as your sword. It's a reminder that leadership is also as much about storytelling as strategy. Her song is one of the oldest recorded pieces of Hebrew poetry, filled with gratitude to God. It celebrates the courage of those who stepped up when the nation needed them most.

Deborah's legacy of courageous leadership left an indelible mark on Israel's history. Her impact wasn't confined to the battlefield; it extended into the hearts and minds of the people. She garnered respect and admiration in a male-dominated society, and her leadership brought about forty years of peace.

The Song of Deborah celebrated a military victory. It enshrined her role as a leader who could bring about change through strength and compassion. Her story continues to inspire, reminding us that leadership is not about gender but the courage to stand up and the wisdom to guide others.

In today's world, Deborah's leadership style offers valuable lessons for all of us, especially women, who find ourselves in influential roles. It's about combining wisdom with decisive action, knowing when to speak and when to listen. Deborah's approach encourages collaborative leadership and mentorship, showing us that the best leaders uplift others. Her story inspires women to step into leadership roles with confidence and vision and to balance spiritual guidance with practical decision-making.

Deeper Insight

Deborah trusted God's promises and inspired others to act on His word, even when the odds seemed impossible. What can you learn from Deborah's confidence in her God-given calling? Are there areas in your life where you need to trust God more fully? How do you think Deborah's leadership style, steady and empowering—can inspire leaders today, whether in families, workplaces, or communities? Sometimes, even strong leaders need encouragement; who in your life might need a "Deborah" moment of encouragement?

Final Thoughts

Leadership is not always about titles or positions; it's about the courage to act when others are paralyzed by fear. I often wonder if I would dare to step up and lead in moments of uncertainty, like Deborah did. Her example challenges me to trust in God's guidance and to be willing to take risks, even when the path isn't clear.

Deborah broke cultural norms, but she didn't do it for herself. She led because God called her to, and she trusted Him to equip her for the task. She also didn't take the fight into her own hands; she empowered Barak to lead the army. Deborah's collaboration with Barak shows that leadership is a shared journey. Her empowerment of him and their final success most likely changed his life. It makes me reflect on how I can support those around me, especially when they face overwhelming challenges. Authentic leadership lifts others and encourages them to succeed.

Deborah's life is a vivid reminder that God's call to lead can come to anyone, regardless of position or conventional expectations. Her story encourages us to embrace our unique roles with courage, wisdom, and humility. Her life is a call to boldly lead, trust your abilities and intuition, and create a legacy of strength and peace. Her story challenges us to rise to the occasion, trust God in the face of challenges, and support others as they do the same. God's got this; now go do your part!

2.4 JAEL: UNEXPECTED HEROISM

It's a warm, dusty afternoon in the tent of a seemingly ordinary woman named Jael. Her story unfolds during Deborah and Barak's time when the Israelites fought to free themselves from Jabin's oppressive rule. Jael was the wife of Heber the Kenite, a group that lived in peace with King Jabin of Canaan, Israel's oppressor. Despite her group's alliance with Jabin, Jael chose to side with the Israelites, God's people, when the opportunity arose. The Kenite's agreement put Jael in a unique position at the time of Sisera's defeat by Deborah and Barak.

The air is still, and the world seems to be holding its breath, on the brink of change. Suddenly, Sisera, the feared Canaanite general, stumbles into her camp, seeking refuge after fleeing his battle with the Israelite army led by Deborah and Barak.

With a calm demeanor, Jael invites him into her tent—a sanctuary amidst chaos. She offers him milk and a place to rest. When he fell asleep, Jael, equipped with only a tent peg and a hammer, dispatched the enemy general with decisive courage.

> Sisera, meanwhile, fled on foot to the tent of Jael, the
> wife of Heber the Kenite, because there was an
> alliance between Jabin king of Hazor and the family
> of Heber the Kenite.
> Jael went out to meet Sisera and said to him, "Come, my
> lord, come right in. Don't be afraid." So he entered
> her tent, and she covered him with a blanket.
> "I'm thirsty," he said. "Please give me some water." She
> opened a skin of milk, gave him a drink, and
> covered him up. "Stand in the doorway of the tent,"
> he told her. "If someone comes by and asks you, 'Is
> anyone in there?' say 'No.'"
> But Jael, Heber's wife, picked up a tent peg and a

hammer and went quietly to him while he lay fast
asleep, exhausted. She drove the peg through his
temple into the ground, and he died.

Just then Barak came by in pursuit of Sisera, and Jael
went out to meet him. "Come," she said, "I will show
you the man you're looking for." So he went in with
her, and there lay Sisera with the tent peg through
his temple—dead.

On that day God subdued Jabin king of Canaan before
the Israelites. And the hand of the Israelites pressed
harder and harder against Jabin king of Canaan
until they destroyed him.

— JUDGES 4:17-24 NIV

Her actions turned the tide of history, proving that heroism often emerges in the most unexpected places. Deborah prophesied that a woman would deliver the final blow in the battle, and Jael became that woman dramatically and surprisingly.

The story of Jael is not without its complexities. On the surface, her actions might seem ruthless, yet they reflect a profound understanding of the stakes involved. The use of deception and violence in her narrative raises ethical questions, challenging our perceptions of morality. Hospitality, a sacred duty in her culture, was strategically balanced with the need to protect her people. Was this a betrayal or a necessary act of war? Each interpretation offers a different lens through which to view her story.

In the biblical and historical context, Jael's decision resonates as both a divine intervention and a shrewd tactical move, illustrating the nuanced nature of justice in times of conflict. Jael's impact on Israel's victory over King Jabin's oppressive regime cannot be overstated. Her single act of bravery marked a turning point in the battle, eliminating a key figure in the Canaanite army.

Though she was a non-combatant, her contribution was celebrated in the Song of Deborah (Please see 2.3 Deborah: Wisdom and Warfare), highlighting her as a pivotal force in Israel's triumph. Her story is a testament to the power of individuals who, despite not being on the front lines, play crucial roles in the larger narrative of victory. In honoring Jael through song, the Israelites acknowledged her courage and strategic insight, recognizing that sometimes the most profound acts of war happen off the battlefield.

Today, Jael's tale inspires us to consider unconventional leadership and the courage to act decisively in situations that defy expectations. Her story reminds us that heroism is not confined to those in positions of power but can be expressed by anyone willing to take bold actions when the moment calls for it.

In our modern context, we often face challenges that require us to step out of our comfort zones and make difficult decisions. Jael's example encourages us to embrace these moments, to trust our instincts, and to recognize that ordinary individuals can achieve extraordinary outcomes. Whether in the boardroom, at home, or in our communities, we are called to lead with the same fearless commitment to what we know is right.

Deeper Insight

Think about Jael's courage to act so boldly against Sisera. What does her story teach us about stepping out of our comfort zones to do what is right? Have you ever faced a situation where you had to take bold action, even though it felt risky or uncomfortable? Are there moments in your life where you felt unqualified even though God called you in unexpected ways? What does Jael's story teach us about trusting God in moments of uncertainty? Have there been times when you hesitated to act, and how might Jael's example inspire you to be more decisive? What does her legacy teach us about the courage to stand for what is right, even when it goes against the expectations of others?

Final Thoughts

Jael's story is a whirlwind of surprise and boldness. Imagine her at that moment—faced with the enemy in her tent, weighing her options, and choosing to act. I think of times when I've hesitated because I wasn't sure I had what it took to step up. Jael's story nudges me to see that sometimes, it's not about being ready; it's about being willing. Her story isn't one of perfection but of purpose. She teaches us that bravery can look different for everyone and that ordinary people can play extraordinary roles in God's plan.

Her actions remind me that God doesn't just call the obvious heroes. He calls the ones willing to trust Him, even when the path ahead is terrifying or unclear. And let's be honest—how many of us would have thought of using a tent peg to make history? Sometimes, the tools we have at hand are perfect for His purpose, even if they are unconventional. Her legacy encourages us to step into opportunities, even if they feel risky or unconventional, trusting that God is at work.

Imagine being plucked from obscurity and suddenly finding yourself in a grand palace with the weight of a nation resting on your shoulders. That's what happened to Esther. She was a Jewish orphan raised by her cousin, Mordecai. She was a beautiful, intelligent, and faithful woman and probably never imagined she would one day be a queen.

Selected for her beauty, when King Xerxes deposed his queen, Vashti, Esther underwent months of preparation, learning the intricacies of palace life while keeping her Jewish identity a secret. Her path to queenship wasn't paved with gold but with courage and faith. The stakes were high, and she had to navigate palace politics with the precision of a tightrope walker. Her Jewish identity, initially hidden, became her strength, a pivotal part of her story that would eventually save her people.

> *When the turn came for Esther (the young woman*
> *Mordecai had adopted, the daughter of his uncle*
> *Abihail) to go to the king, she asked for nothing*
> *other than what Hegai, the king's eunuch who was*
> *in charge of the harem, suggested. And Esther won*
> *the favor of everyone who saw her. She was taken*
> *to King Xerxes in the royal residence in the tenth*
> *month, the month of Tebeth, in the seventh year of*
> *his reign.*

Now the king was attracted to Esther more than to any
of the other women, and she won his favor and
approval more than any of the other virgins. So he
set a royal crown on her head and made her queen
instead of Vashti. And the king gave a great
banquet, Esther's banquet, for all his nobles and
officials. He proclaimed a holiday throughout the
provinces and distributed gifts with royal liberality.

— ESTHER 2:15-18 NIV

Esther was chosen to be queen, but she kept her Jewish identity a secret. Mordecai, her cousin, Mordecai's, had forbidden her to reveal her family background and nationality. After Mordecai had discovered a plot to assassinate King Xerxes, Haman was elevated above all the other nobles. Due to this elevation, all the royal officials knelt to honor Haman. When Mordecai refused to kneel or pay honor to Haman, Haman became enraged. Seeking revenge, Haman, now a high-ranking official in Xerxes' court, devised a plan to destroy all the Jews in the empire. Using deceit, Haman convinced Xerxes to issue a decree for their extermination.

When Mordecai learned of all that had been done, he
tore his clothes, put on sackcloth and ashes, and
went out into the city, wailing loudly and bitterly.
But he went only as far as the king's gate, because
no one clothed in sackcloth was allowed to enter it.
In every province to which the edict and order of the
king came, there was great mourning among the
Jews, with fasting, weeping and wailing. Many lay
in sackcloth and ashes.
When Esther's eunuchs and female attendants came
and told her about Mordecai, she was in great

distress. She sent clothes for him to put on instead of his sackcloth, but he would not accept them. Then Esther summoned Hathak, one of the king's eunuchs assigned to attend her, and ordered him to find out what was troubling Mordecai and why.

So Hathak went out to Mordecai in the open square of the city in front of the king's gate. Mordecai told him everything that had happened to him, including the exact amount of money Haman had promised to pay into the royal treasury for the destruction of the Jews. He also gave him a copy of the text of the edict for their annihilation, which had been published in Susa, to show to Esther and explain it to her, and he told him to instruct her to go into the king's presence to beg for mercy and plead with him for her people.

— ESTHER 4:1-8 NIV

When the decree threatened the very existence of her people, Esther called upon the power of prayer and fasting. Her actions weren't just a personal endeavor but a communal call to intercession. She knew that approaching the king uninvited could cost her life. Still, rather than act immediately, she chose patience and timing.

She instructed him to say to Mordecai, "All the king's officials and the people of the royal provinces know that for any man or woman who approaches the king in the inner court without being summoned the king has but one law: that they be put to death unless the king extends the gold scepter to them and spares their lives. But thirty days have passed since I was called to go to the king."

When Esther's words were reported to Mordecai, he sent

back this answer: "Do not think that because you
are in the king's house you alone of all the Jews will
escape. For if you remain silent at this time, relief
and deliverance for the Jews will arise from another
place, but you and your father's family will perish.
And who knows but that you have come to your
royal position for such a time as this?"
Then Esther sent this reply to Mordecai: "Go, gather
together all the Jews who are in Susa, and fast for
me. Do not eat or drink for three days, night or day.
I and my attendants will fast as you do. When this
is done, I will go to the king, even though it is
against the law. And if I perish, I perish."

— ESTHER 4:10-16 NIV

Esther's request was about something other than rushing into the king's presence with demands. Royal law stated that no one, not even the queen, could approach the king without being summoned. Instead, she orchestrated a series of banquets, each delay building anticipation and softening the king's heart.

They were private banquets; only the king and Haman were invited, allowing Ester to control the conversation. At the first banquet, the king was willing to grant her a great favor, but instead of making a request, she invited him and Haman to a second banquet the next day. This strategic pause allowed her to reveal Haman's plot at the right moment, ensuring maximum impact.

She set the perfect trap for Haman. Full of pride and arrogance, Haman left the first banquet feeling special and consequential. The delay gave time for events to unfold, leading to his downfall.

So the king and Haman went to Queen Esther's
  banquet, and as they were drinking wine on the
  second day, the king again asked, "Queen Esther,
  what is your petition? It will be given you. What is
  your request? Even up to half the kingdom, it will be
  granted."
Then Queen Esther answered, "If I have found favor
  with you, Your Majesty, and if it pleases you, grant
  me my life—this is my petition. And spare my
  people—this is my request. For I and my people have
  been sold to be destroyed, killed and annihilated. If
  we had merely been sold as male and female slaves,
  I would have kept quiet, because no such distress
  would justify disturbing the king."
King Xerxes asked Queen Esther, "Who is he? Where is
  he—the man who has dared to do such a thing?"
Esther said, "An adversary and enemy! This vile
  Haman!"

— ESTHER 7:1-6 NIV

The king was shocked and enraged. He stormed out in anger, and Haman threw himself at Esther, begging for his life—a huge mistake because when the king returned, he thought Haman was attacking the queen!

The king exclaimed, "Will he even molest the queen
  while she is with me in the house?"

— ESTHER 7:8 NIV

Haman was immediately sentenced to death and impaled on the pole he had set up for Mordecai outside his house.

Esther's courage to intervene was a defining moment. It wasn't just about saving her own skin but risking everything for her people. The pivotal moment came when she entered the king's throne room uninvited. Her heart must have been pounding with each step, yet she stood firm, a testament to the power of fasting and prayer. Esther's bravery and strategic acumen shone through as she carefully unveiled Haman's plot during the banquets. Her story reminds us that the most courageous acts sometimes involve quiet strength and calculated risks, even when the consequences loom large.

Her leadership didn't stop at revealing the plot. Esther's influence on the king led to the reversal of the deadly edict, saving countless lives and establishing the festival of Purim—a celebration of deliverance that endures today. Her actions cemented her position as a queen and a savior of her people. Esther's story is woven into the cultural memory of the Jewish people, a legacy of courage and faith that continues to inspire.

In today's world, Esther's strategic influence offers valuable lessons in leveraging our opportunities. Strategic planning is key in advocacy efforts, reminding us to be thoughtful and deliberate in our actions. Esther's story encourages us to have confidence and courage in taking calculated risks and using our positions for the greater good, especially during times of crisis.

It's about balancing personal identity with leadership responsibilities, ensuring our actions align with our values. By doing so, we can use our platforms to effect positive change, just as Esther did. Her life is a beacon guiding us to act with courage, wisdom, and an unwavering commitment to justice.

Deeper Insight

Reflect on a moment you felt called to step up for a greater purpose. Does Esther's willingness to risk her life for her people inspire you to face challenges in your own life? What does her story teach us about finding courage when unprepared or afraid? Mordecai believed Esther's position as queen was part of God's plan. Does her story encourage you to trust that God is working in your life, even when you can't see it? How does Esther's example challenge you to use your influence, however small, to help others? What does her story teach us about balancing faith and action, trusting God while doing our part?

Final Thoughts

I'm a problem solver, and I want to act immediately when I see a problem. Esther teaches me that waiting, preparing, and trusting God's timing is often the wiser approach. God's timing frequently differs from ours, but when we trust Him, He works everything out for good. Next time you're tempted to rush into action, remember Esther, the queen who waited for the right moment—and saved a nation.

Esther's story is about faith, courage, and stepping into God's purpose. Imagine the fear she must have felt walking into the throne room, knowing she could be killed for approaching the king uninvited, but she did it anyway. She teaches us that faith is about moving forward, even when you're scared. Don't forget Mordecai's words - "for such a time as this." That phrase sticks with me. It reminds me that every moment, every challenge, and every opportunity has a purpose in God's plan.

Reflections on Courage and Leadership

Closing this chapter, I think about how strong and brave these women were: Esther saving her people, Miriam leading her people through the Red Sea out of Egypt, Shiprah and Puah defying Pharoah, Deborah devising a plan for battle and leading it, and Jael calmly dispatching a much-feared Canaanite general.

Their actions may seem simple, but we all know how personal history provides context for each decision. Biblical leaders often faced situations that required extraordinary courage. Their ability to lead came from trusting God's promise and powers. Courage isn't always loud or public; sometimes, it's quiet defiance in the face of injustice, choosing what is right, even if it's difficult or dangerous. True courage starts with the confidence that God is with us, equipping us to face any challenge. When we boldly lead, we encourage others to step out in faith.

The women in this chapter made difficult choices, trusting God was in control. While these women made choices that seemed miraculous now, they still experienced jealousy, pride, and fear and had to overcome ordinary challenges. They still needed to practice humility and a deep trust in God. We, too, need to trust that God is weaving our story into His greater plan, even though we can't see the whole picture. Whether leading a family, a team, or a community, let's step out boldly, act humbly, serve with love, and trust God to work through us for His purposes.

LOVE AND LOYALTY

3.1 RUTH: DEVOTION BEYOND BORDERS

Have you ever been at a crossroads, with your entire future on the line, trying to decide which way to go? Ruth, a recently widowed woman from Moab, faced a decision for her future that would alter the course of history. Her mother-in-law, Naomi, was preparing to return to Bethlehem after the death of her husband and sons left them both vulnerable.

The backdrop of Ruth's story is one of struggle and resilience. Ruth was a Moabite woman who married into an Israelite family. Her mother-in-law, Naomi, Naomi's husband, and their sons had fled to Moab due to famine, only for tragedy to strike. Ruth's husband, along with her father-in-law and brother-in-law, died while she was still young.

Rather than returning to her family and starting over, Ruth remained with her mother-in-law, Naomi, committing herself to Naomi and the God of Israel. Left with little more than each other, Ruth's decision to follow Naomi back to Bethlehem was a profound act of loyalty. Moab was her home, where she was born and raised, yet she chose to leave it all behind.

Ruth's choice was not just about geography but also about loyalty, courage, and faith. Even though Naomi urged Ruth and her sister-in-law, Orpah, to return to their families, Ruth made a bold and heartfelt decision.

> *"Look," said Naomi, "your sister-in-law is going back to her people and her gods. Go back with her."*
> *But Ruth replied, "Don't urge me to leave you or to turn back from you. Where you go I will go, and where you stay I will stay. Your people will be my people and your God my God. Where you die I will die, and there I will be buried. May the Lord deal with me, be it ever so severely, if even death separates you and me." When Naomi realized that Ruth was determined to go with her, she stopped urging her.*

— RUTH 1:16 NIV

These words were more than a pledge; they were a covenant of love and faith, transcending cultural norms and personal sacrifice. Her statements weren't just a move but a leap of faith into the unknown, embracing a new culture and religion with open arms.

Ruth's choice to leave her homeland and people behind illustrates her loyalty to Naomi and her commitment to a new life and a new God. Naomi was an unhappy and bitter woman, making Ruth's commitment to stay with her surprising. Her journey to Bethlehem was a physical and spiritual migration, marking the beginning of an extraordinary story.

Ruth's adaptation to her new life in Bethlehem was a testament to her resilience and faith. They arrived just in time for the barley harvest. Ruth took the initiative to glean in the fields to provide for herself and Naomi. Her willingness to glean in the fields, a practice reserved for the poor and marginalized, demonstrated her dedication to provide for Naomi and herself in a manner that adhered to God's law. By chance—or divine providence—she ended up in the fields of Boaz, a kind and wealthy relative of Naomi. Boaz noticed Ruth's diligence and kindness and offered her protection and provision.

Embracing Israel's customs and religious practices, she quickly became a part of the community. Despite initially being an outsider, Ruth's hard work and humility earned her the respect and acceptance of those around her. The community's acceptance of Ruth was not just a social formality but a reflection of God's inclusive love and grace, a theme that resonates through her story and into our lives today.

Following Naomi's guidance, Ruth found favor with Boaz, a man of standing in Bethlehem, who became her kinsman-redeemer. The kinsman-redeemer played a pivotal role in Hebrew culture, ensuring the continuation of family lineage. Their marriage was not only a personal union but a divine appointment that would place Ruth in the genealogy of Jesus, as recorded in Matthew 1.

> *Salmon the father of Boaz, whose mother was Rahab,*
> *Boaz the father of Obed, whose mother was Ruth,*
> *Obed the father of Jesse, and Jesse the father of King*
> *David.*

> — MATTHEW 1:5-6 NIV

Ruth's story is a testament to how acts of faith and devotion, even in the seemingly mundane, can be integral to God's extraordinary plan of salvation. In marrying Boaz and giving birth to Obed, the grandfather of King David, Ruth's legacy became one of redemption and hope. Ruth, a foreigner and widow, became part of God's grand story of redemption, showing His love and inclusion of all people.

Ruth's story offers us timeless lessons in loyalty and love, transcending cultural and personal boundaries. Her commitment to Naomi encourages us to foster loyalty and faithfulness in our own familial bonds. In a world that often feels fragmented, Ruth's example reminds us of the power of love to bridge divides and foster unity. Her life challenges us to embrace change with faith and loyalty, trusting that where we are led, God's purpose will follow.

Whether adapting to new circumstances or standing by loved ones in times of need, Ruth's story inspires us to live out our faith with courage and devotion. Her legacy calls us to act with integrity and love, confident that even our most minor acts of loyalty can play a role in a much grander divine tapestry. Ruth's role in God's grand narrative is as significant as it is unexpected. Her unwavering loyalty positioned her within the lineage of David and, ultimately, Jesus Christ.

Deeper Insight

Reflect on how you can express Ruth's commitment to those you love, even when the path is uncertain. Have you ever faced a decision where choosing loyalty required personal sacrifice? How did it impact you? Are there people in your life who need your support and commitment right now? What small steps of faith can you take today to move closer to God's purposes for your life? How can you trust Him in the day-to-day challenges of life? Ruth's story shows how God brought beauty from brokenness. Does her story inspire you to find hope in your own challenges? What bold step might God be calling you to take?

Final Thoughts

I've always admired Ruth's courage and faith. Leaving everything familiar to follow Naomi must have been terrifying, but she trusted in a future with Naomi. Her story reminds me that faith often requires taking risks and stepping into the unknown, trusting that God is guiding the way. Her faith, courage, and love inspire us to trust God and live with the same steadfast heart.

I also love how Ruth's story reminds us that God's plans often unfold in quiet, everyday moments. Her story is about more than loyalty or hard work; it's about how God brings beauty and hope out of brokenness. Whether we feel like outsiders, face difficult circumstances, or wonder if God sees us in the mundane moments of life, Ruth reminds us that God is always working. Her faith, courage, and love inspire us to trust God and live with the same steadfast heart.

Hannah was married to Elkanah, who loved her deeply. She was happy in her marriage, but she seemed unable to have children. A woman deeply burdened by longing for a child, Hannah stood amidst the crowd at Shiloh. She made the pilgrimage every year, carrying the weight of unmet hopes. Her rival, Peninnah, Elkanah's other wife, frequently reminded her of her barrenness, a source of deep emotional pain.

The rivalry was more than just petty jealousy; it was a daily reminder of what Hannah lacked. At Shiloh, her heart broke open, and she succumbed to a flood of tears, and she poured out her soul before God. Her prayer was not just a request but a desperate plea, a raw and honest cry for a child. Her prayer was so intense the priest Eli thought she was drunk. She promised if God granted her a son, she would dedicate him back to the Lord —a vow of profound faith and commitment.

> *In her deep anguish Hannah prayed to the Lord, weeping bitterly. And she made a vow, saying, "Lord Almighty, if you will only look on your servant's misery and remember me, and not forget your servant but give her a son, then I will give him to the Lord for all the days of his life, and no razor will ever be used on his head."*
> *As she kept on praying to the Lord, Eli observed her mouth. Hannah was praying in her heart, and her lips were moving but her voice was not heard. Eli thought she was drunk and said to her, "How long are you going to stay drunk? Put away your wine." "Not so, my lord," Hannah replied, "I am a woman who is deeply troubled. I have not been drinking wine or beer; I was pouring out my soul to the Lord. Do not take your servant for a wicked woman; I*

*have been praying here out of my great anguish and
grief."*

*Eli answered, "Go in peace, and may the God of Israel
grant you what you have asked of him."*

— 1 SAMUEL 1:10-17 NIV

Then came the day Hannah's prayers were answered. She gave birth to Samuel, whose name means "heard by God." Samuel's birth was a testament to His answer to her prayers. The joy of this answered prayer rippled through her life and into her community. Hannah didn't just celebrate quietly; she returned to the temple to fulfill her vow, dedicating Samuel to God's service. Her song of thanksgiving, recorded in 1 Samuel 2, was a poetic reflection of her gratitude and faith. It wasn't just a song; it was a declaration of God's faithfulness and a testament to the power of persistent prayer.

Hannah's Song of Praise (1 Samuel 2:1-11 NIV)

*Then Hannah prayed and said: "My heart rejoices in
the Lord; in the Lord my horn is lifted high.
My mouth boasts over my enemies, for I delight in your
deliverance.*

*"There is no one holy like the Lord; there is no one
besides you; there is no Rock like our God.*

*"Do not keep talking so proudly or let your mouth speak
such arrogance, for the Lord is a God who knows,
and by him deeds are weighed.*

*"The bows of the warriors are broken, but those who
stumbled are armed with strength.*

Those who were full hire themselves out for food, but
those who were hungry are hungry no more.
She who was barren has borne seven children, but she
who has had many sons pines away.

"The Lord brings death and makes alive; he brings
down to the grave and raises up.
The Lord sends poverty and wealth; he humbles and he
exalts.
He raises the poor from the dust and lifts the needy
from the ash heap; he seats them with princes and
has them inherit a throne of honor.

"For the foundations of the earth are the Lord's; on
them he has set the world.
He will guard the feet of his faithful servants, but the
wicked will be silenced in the place of darkness.

"It is not by strength that one prevails; those who oppose
the Lord will be broken.
The Most High will thunder from heaven; the Lord will
judge the ends of the earth.

"He will give strength to his king and exalt the horn of
his anointed."

Then Elkanah went home to Ramah, but the boy minis-
tered before the Lord under Eli the priest.

— 1 SAMUEL 2:1-11 NIV

Imagine the strength it took for Hannah to leave Samuel at the
temple under Eli's care. It was an act of incredible faith and selflessness, fulfilling her promise to God. Her dedication to

Samuel wasn't just a symbolic gesture but a tangible act of trust in God's plan for her son. Samuel grew to become one of Israel's greatest prophets and leaders, shaping the spiritual and political landscape of his time. Hannah's influence on Samuel's upbringing was profound, rooted in the love and faith that had brought him into the world.

Hannah's hymn of thanksgiving is rich with theological depth, touching on themes of reversal and divine justice. Her song parallels Mary's Magnificat, highlighting God's intervention in the lives of the humble and faithful. Both songs celebrate God's sovereignty and justice, emphasizing that He lifts the lowly and humbles the proud. Hannah reminds us that God's ways often defy human expectations, bringing hope and justice where there seems to be none.

In our lives today, Hannah's example encourages us to persevere in prayer. Her story reminds us that prayer is not just about asking; it's about building a relationship with God and trusting Him with our deepest desires. Her story teaches us the importance of fulfilling our promises and commitments, even when they require sacrifice. It's about cultivating a life of faith and hope, knowing that God hears and answers in His perfect timing.

Hannah's life calls us to remember and be thankful for our blessings and to recognize God's hand in the everyday moments of grace and provision. Her journey of faith and fulfillment inspires us to hold onto hope, trusting that God's plans for us are good, even when the path is unclear.

Deeper Insight

Hannah's desperate plea reminds us we can bring our deepest pains and desires to God without fear. Her story illustrates that heartfelt, persistent prayer can lead to incredible outcomes, even when the wait feels unbearable. Does Hannah's example encourage you to bring your deepest desires and struggles to God in prayer? Have you ever experienced a season of waiting where you needed to trust God's timing? What steps can you take to deepen your trust in God, even when prayers seem unanswered? Hannah surrendered her greatest blessing—her son—to God. Are there areas in your life where you need to let go and trust God with the outcome? What blessings can you thank God for today, even if some prayers remain unanswered?

Final Thoughts

Hannah's story resonates deeply with me because it's so real and raw. Her vulnerability in prayer reminds me that it's okay to bring all our emotions to God—the heartbreak, the frustration, and even the doubts. Her faith is inspiring. She didn't just ask God for a miracle; she trusted Him completely, even when it meant giving up what she wanted most.

Hannah's heartfelt prayer reminds us that God listens to the cries of His people. Even when we feel overlooked or forgotten, God is attentive to our needs. Nor did she let her sorrow turn her away from God. Instead, she leaned into her faith, trusting Him with her deepest desires. Hannah's willingness to dedicate Samuel to God shows her trust and gratitude. She recognized that her blessing was God's and gave back to Him with an open heart.

Hannah's story reminds us that God's timing and purposes are always good, even when they don't align with our expectations. We can all learn from Hannah's journey. Whether we're waiting on God for something or looking for ways to honor Him, prayer, trust, and praise are all part of the journey. She's a testament to what happens when we surrender to God and trust Him to work in His perfect way.

Michal must have first seen David, the shepherd turned hero, in the bustling corridors of King Saul's palace. It was a time of triumph and celebration, with David fresh from his victory over Goliath. Michal, Saul's daughter, was smitten. Their love story begins with romance but soon becomes entangled in the political drama surrounding Saul's court.

Michal's initial love for David was fierce and protective. David had entered Saul's service as a musician to soothe Saul's troubled spirit. After David defeated Goliath, the women of Israel sang a song that compared David and Saul.

> "Saul has slain his thousands, and David his tens of
> thousands."
>
> — 1 SAMUEL 18:7 NIV

This comparison infuriated Saul and planted the seeds of jealousy in his heart. In his paranoia, Saul started to see David as a threat to his throne. Michal learns of Saul's plan to kill David and helps him escape from her father's murderous intent by letting him down through a window, a daring act that saves his life.

> Saul sent men to David's house to watch it and to kill
> him in the morning. But Michal, David's wife,
> warned him, "If you don't run for your life tonight,
> tomorrow you'll be killed." So Michal let David
> down through a window, and he fled and escaped.
> Then Michal took an idol and laid it on the bed,
> covering it with a garment and putting some goats'
> hair at the head.

When Saul sent the men to capture David, Michal said,
"He is ill."
Then Saul sent the men back to see David and told
them, "Bring him up to me in his bed so that I may
kill him." But when the men entered, there was the
idol in the bed, and at the head was some goats'
hair.
Saul said to Michal, "Why did you deceive me like this
and send my enemy away so that he escaped?"
Michal told him, "He said to me, 'Let me get away.
Why should I kill you?'"

— 1 SAMUEL 19:11-17 NIV

This moment was a testament to her loyalty and courage. Still, it was also the beginning of a complex relationship that would be tested by ambition, betrayal, and power.

As time passed, Michal's relationship with David became more tangled. After helping him flee, she was left behind and eventually given in marriage to another man, Paltiel, by her father, Saul. This act was as much a political maneuver as a personal betrayal.

The separation between David and Michal was physical and emotional, straining the bonds of love that had once been so strong. When David rose to power, he demanded Michal's return as a condition for his kingship.

Then Abner sent messengers on his behalf to say to
David, "Whose land is it? Make an agreement with
me, and I will help you bring all Israel over to you."
"Good," said David. "I will make an agreement with
you. But I demand one thing of you: Do not come
into my presence unless you bring Michal daughter

of Saul when you come to see me." Then David sent
messengers to Ish-Bosheth son of Saul, demanding,
"Give me my wife Michal, whom I betrothed to
myself for the price of a hundred Philistine
foreskins."

— 2 SAMUEL 3:12-14 NIV

This move was more political than romantic, and his tone is very much lacking in romance. Imagine the conflict in Michal's heart, torn between her past love and her present reality. Her current husband, Paltiel, loved her and followed her to David, although he was sent back home. Her reunion with David was overshadowed by the politics of power, and the love that once burned bright was now clouded by ambition and loss.

Michal's life was defined by her role as a political pawn, used to cement alliances and exert influence. Her marriage to David was more than a union of love; it was a strategic alliance crucial in the volatile world of ancient Israelite politics. Yet, this role came at a cost. The emotional impact of being separated from David, used by her father, and then reclaimed by David left its scars.

Her life was a series of personal losses, each more profound than the last, illustrating the painful intersection of love and power. Michal's experience speaks to the complexities of navigating personal ambitions and emotional needs within a world that often sees individuals as mere chess pieces in a larger game.

Michal's legacy is one of love and tragedy intertwined. Her story unfolds as a narrative of what could have been, overshadowed by bitterness and the harsh realities of royal life and war. This bitterness is poignantly expressed in her confrontation with David in 2 Samuel 6, where she criticizes him for his exuberant dancing before the Ark of the Covenant.

When David returned home to bless his household,
Michal daughter of Saul came out to meet him and
said, "How the king of Israel has distinguished
himself today, going around half-naked in full view
of the slave girls of his servants as any vulgar fellow
would!"
David said to Michal, "It was before the Lord, who
chose me rather than your father or anyone from
his house when he appointed me ruler over the
Lord's people Israel—I will celebrate before the Lord.
I will become even more undignified than this, and I
will be humiliated in my own eyes. But by these
slave girls you spoke of, I will be held in honor."
And Michal daughter of Saul had no children to the day
of her death.

— 2 SAMUEL 6:20-23 NIV

Her words are steeped in the pain of lost dreams and unmet expectations. Despite her royal status, Michal's absence from the lineage of David's successors underscores the tragic elements of her life, highlighting how personal and political dynamics can shape one's legacy in ways that leave one feeling both powerful and powerless. Michal did not have any children; this is often interpreted as a sign of her isolation or God's judgment.

Today, Michal's story offers insights into the delicate balance of love, loyalty, and personal ambition. It challenges us to navigate the complexities of our relationships, understanding that love can be both a source of strength and vulnerability. Michal's life reminds us that familial and political contexts can profoundly influence our personal journeys, shaping our choices and their consequences. Her story invites reflection on how we manage our ambitions and emotional needs, urging us to seek harmony between the two. Ultimately, Michal's life is a testament to the enduring struggle to find one's voice and place in a world that often demands more than we are willing or to give.

Deeper Insight

Michal's bitterness toward David seems rooted in her unresolved pain. Are there areas in your life where bitterness has taken root? Does her story encourage you to confront and release resentment before it damages relationships? Are there relationships in your life where forgiveness or understanding is needed? What steps can you take to cultivate forgiveness and peace? Michal was repeatedly caught in situations she didn't choose. How do you respond when life feels unfair? Have you considered that taking the high road in unfair situations may be a part of God's plan? Michal's bravery in saving David is inspiring, but her later life shows a struggle to maintain that courage in other circumstances. How do you find strength in difficult moments?

Final Thoughts

Michal's life is like a drama, full of love, betrayal, and heartbreak. I imagine her as a young woman, excited and hopeful about her marriage to David, only to see that hope eroded by political games and personal conflicts. It's easy to feel frustrated on her behalf—her life was shaped so much by the choices of others. Sometimes, I've felt deeply connected to someone, only to face the harsh reality of disappointment later. Michal's early courage and love inspire me, while her later pain reminds me that even the most profound relationships can be fraught with challenges.

Her story encourages me to examine my expectations of others and to strive for honest communication in my relationships. How often have I struggled to balance love and loyalty with the realities of life? Life is messy, relationships are complicated, and faith doesn't always come easily.

Michal's story reminds us to find courage, seek healing, and trust God even when life feels overwhelming. It also challenges us to seek healing where bitterness has taken root and to remember that even when things don't turn out as we'd hoped, there is value in the journey itself.

Michal's narrative is a vivid reminder that love, loyalty, and human emotion are complex and often contradictory. Her life, marked by both brave acts of devotion and deep personal sorrow, challenges us to confront our struggles with expectation, disappointment, and the need for forgiveness. I hope her story encourages you to embrace the full spectrum of your feelings, seek resolution and healing, and remember that every relationship carries the potential for growth—even amid heartache.

Abigail was an intelligent and beautiful woman but her husband was surly and mean in his dealings...

— 1 SAMUEL 25:3 NIV

Wow, does that one verse spell out a story or what? Abigail was married to Nabal, whose name literally means "fool." He lived up to his name when David sent messengers to Nabal asking for provisions. David and his men were protecting Nabal's shepherds during sheep-shearing time in the wilderness. Nabal insulted them and refused. Justifiably angered, David, the future king, marches towards Nabal's estate with thoughts of vengeance. Abigail, a woman of remarkable wisdom and grace, sees the brewing disaster. She acts with the urgency of a mother catching a child about to tumble.

Her quick thinking is nothing short of remarkable. In a situation where many would freeze or panic, she springs into action. Abigail gathers an impressive offering—bread, wine, sheep, and figs—and sets out to meet David. Her gifts are not mere tokens; they're strategic olive branches aimed at diffusing the hostility that could lead to unnecessary bloodshed. Imagine her riding towards David, knowing full well the risk she takes. Her strategic timing is impeccable, intercepting him at the right moment to prevent a catastrophe.

As she approaches David, Abigail's eloquence shines. She dismounts, bows low, and delivers a humble and persuasive speech. In 1 Samuel 25, her words flow with a blend of humility and authority, appealing to David's sense of justice and mercy. She acknowledges the folly of her husband, Nabal. She redirects David's focus to his greater destiny. Abigail also reminds David of his future kingship, urging him to avoid the stain of unnecessary bloodshed on his conscience. Her ability to speak truth to power with such finesse is a masterclass in diplomacy. She doesn't scold or demand; instead, she appeals to David's better nature, weaving a narrative that aligns with his vision and values.

> When Abigail saw David, she quickly got off her donkey and bowed down before David with her face to the ground. She fell at his feet and said: "Pardon your servant, my Lord, and let me speak to you; hear what your servant has to say. Please pay no attention, my Lord, to that wicked man Nabal. He is just like his name—his name means Fool, and folly goes with him. And as for me, your servant, I did not see the men my Lord sent. And now, my Lord, as surely as the Lord your God lives and as you live, since the Lord has kept you from bloodshed and from avenging yourself with your own hands, may your enemies and all who are intent on harming my Lord be like Nabal. And let this gift, which your servant has brought to my Lord, be given to the men who follow you.
>
> — 1 SAMUEL 25:23-27 NIV

Abigail's words moved David. He praised her for her wisdom and for preventing him from making a rash decision.

> David said to Abigail, "Praise be to the Lord, the God of Israel, who has sent you today to meet me. May you be blessed for your good judgment and for keeping me from bloodshed this day and from avenging myself with my own hands. Otherwise, as surely as the Lord, the God of Israel, lives, who has kept me

from harming you, if you had not come quickly to
meet me, not one male belonging to Nabal would
have been left alive by daybreak." Then David
accepted from her hand what she had brought him
and said, "Go home in peace. I have heard your
words and granted your request."

— 1 SAMUEL 25:32-35 NIV

Abigail's role as a wise counselor becomes evident in the contrast between her and Nabal. While Nabal's actions are reckless and self-serving, Abigail's are calculated and selfless. Abigail's intervention prevented violence and left a lasting impact on David's decision-making, reinforcing the value of measured responses over impulsive actions. Not long after, Nabal died, and Abigail became David's wife.

Her subsequent marriage to David is a testament to her strength of character and the respect she garnered through her actions. This alliance wasn't just about joining two individuals; it symbolized the merging of wisdom and leadership, a partnership supporting David's future reign.

Her actions reflect practical, timeless leadership qualities. Abigail exemplifies the balance of assertiveness with respect, showing that one can be firm and diplomatic. She reminds us that a calm and thoughtful response can often avert disaster. Her ability to navigate complex interpersonal dynamics serves as a reminder that leadership is not about force but influence.

In today's world, Abigail's peacemaking skills are lessons in conflict resolution. Her story encourages us to approach disputes with wisdom and diplomacy and practice thoughtful communication and negotiation in both personal and professional relationships. By embracing proactive peacebuilding, we can foster environments where understanding and cooperation prevail over discord.

Abigail's narrative inspires us to pause, consider, and act with intention in a world often quick to anger. Her legacy urges us to be peacemakers in our areas of influence, meeting conflict with calm and transforming potential crises into opportunities for reconciliation. Whether in our homes, workplaces, or communities, we're called to channel her wisdom and courage, ensuring that our actions leave a mark of peace and understanding.

Deeper Insight

How does Abigail's quick and thoughtful response challenge you to approach conflict with wisdom? Are there situations where you need to pause, assess, and act with greater discernment? What steps can you take to cultivate wisdom in your daily decisions? Have you ever been part of a situation where calm words and actions resolved a conflict? What can you learn from that experience? Does her story encourage you to trust God with difficult people or situations? How can you bring God's peace into tense or challenging circumstances? How can her example inspire you to remain faithful and strong in your challenges?

Final Thoughts

Abigail's story speaks to me on many levels. There have been moments in my life when anger threatened to overwhelm me—times when the easy path was to react impulsively rather than pause and reflect. Abigail reminds me that true strength lies in measured action and choosing a path of peace and wisdom. This may require taking a deep breath and pausing to consider the bigger picture. Her courage inspires me to look beyond my frustrations and see the bigger picture, trusting that God's plan is more significant than any immediate conflict.

Her example also encourages me to protect and uplift those around me, even when it's not my responsibility. It reminds me that our actions, no matter how small, can have a lasting impact on others and that sometimes, a gentle word can prevent a great tragedy.

Abigail's life is a testament to the power of a wise and courageous heart. Her story challenges us to be peacemakers, to act with humility and determination, and to trust that God honors those who seek to do His will. I hope her example inspires you to reflect on how you handle conflict, seek wisdom in every situation, and extend grace and protection to those in need.

3.5 RIZPAH: A MOTHER'S LOVE AND VIGIL

Picture a mother standing alone on a barren hill, her eyes fixed on the bodies of her sons. Rizpah's story is both heartbreaking and inspiring. It occurred during a dark and troubling time in Israel's history when King David sought to end a three-year famine.

The Lord revealed that the famine resulted from Saul's actions against the Gibeonites, whom he had wronged by breaking a treaty. To atone for this injustice, the Gibeonites requested the execution of seven of Saul's male descendants. David agreed, and Rizpah's two sons, Armoni and Mephibosheth, along with five others, were handed over and executed. Their bodies were left on a hill, exposed.

Rizpah was a concubine of King Saul. Their sons, executed by the Gibeonites, were left exposed, a dishonorable fate in ancient Israelite culture. Rizpah took sackcloth and made a makeshift shelter on a rock near their bodies. Rizpah, in her grief, refused to let their memory fade. She began a vigil, a solitary watch over her sons' bodies, protecting them from scavengers and the elements for months on end.

Her love was fierce, her dedication unwavering. Under the scorching sun and through cold nights, Rizpah stood guard, armed with nothing but a sackcloth spread on a rock and a mother's unyielding love. Imagine the physical and emotional toll this took. Yet, she remained a silent testament to the depth of maternal devotion and the power of love to transcend even the darkest of circumstances.

Rizpah's actions speak volumes about sacrificial love and commitment. Her vigil was not just an act of mourning; it was a profound statement of defiance against injustice and neglect. It demonstrated that even in the face of death, love endures. Her perseverance highlighted the dignity she sought for her sons, ensuring that they were not forgotten by the world that had so carelessly discarded them.

Rizpah's devotion was a quiet rebellion for the sons she had lost, a way of reclaiming some measure of respect and humanity for them. Her steadfast presence showed that love is not passive; it is active and demanding, and at times, it asks more of us than we think we can give. But in giving, we find strength we never knew we had. Rizpah's love was as relentless as the sun that beat down upon her, and this love stirred the hearts of those who witnessed her vigil.

The impact of Rizpah's actions rippled through her community and reached the ears of King David himself. Moved by her unwavering dedication, he was compelled to act. David ordered that the bones of her sons, along with those of Saul and Jonathan, be gathered and given a proper burial.

> *Rizpah daughter of Aiah took sackcloth and spread it out for herself on a rock. From the beginning of the harvest till the rain poured down from the heavens on the bodies, she did not let the birds touch them by day or the wild animals by night. When David was told what Aiah's daughter Rizpah, Saul's concubine, had done, he went and took the bones of Saul and his son Jonathan from the citizens of Jabesh Gilead. (They had stolen their bodies from the public square at Beth Shan, where the Philistines had hung them after they struck Saul down on Gilboa.) David brought the bones of Saul and his son Jonathan from there, and the bones of those who had been killed and exposed were gathered up.*
> *They buried the bones of Saul and his son Jonathan in the tomb of Saul's father Kish, at Zela in Benjamin,*

and did everything the king commanded. After that,
God answered prayer in behalf of the land.

— 2 SAMUEL 21:10-14 NIV

This act of justice and respect directly responded to Rizpah's silent plea. Though born of personal grief, her vigil became a powerful catalyst for change, prompting a king to right a wrong. He retrieved the remains of Saul, Jonathan, and the seven men who had been executed and gave them a proper burial in the family tomb. This act of honor brought closure to the tragic situation, and God ended the famine afterward.

Rizpah's story reminds us that sometimes, the most profound actions don't come from a place of power but from a place of love and loss. Her steadfast vigil was a testament to the impact of a mother's love, showing that even silent acts from the powerless can move the hearts of the powerful.

In today's world, Rizpah's story offers a poignant lesson in love and advocacy. Mourning can be an act of advocacy, a way to honor those we have lost and to demand justice in their name. Her story challenges us to speak up for those who cannot speak for themselves, to stand firm in the face of injustice, and to let our love be a driving force for change.

Her actions demonstrate that love is a feeling and a commitment to act, protect, and honor those we hold dear. In our own lives, we can take inspiration from Rizpah by standing up for our loved ones, advocating for their needs, and ensuring their dignity is respected. Her legacy calls us to love fiercely and to let that love guide our actions, even when the world seems indifferent to our pain.

Deeper Insight

Rizpah's love for her sons compelled her to guard their bodies for months. Does her example inspire you to act selflessly for those you love? Rizpah channeled her sorrow into action. Can you use your pain to bring about positive change or healing? In what ways can you support someone experiencing grief, offering them the dignity and care they need? Have you ever witnessed an act of quiet persistence that led to meaningful change? What steps can you take to advocate for someone who cannot speak up for themselves?

Final Thoughts

Rizpah's story touches me because it's so raw and honest. Though her role in the Bible is small in terms of verses, her actions have a powerful impact, showing the depth of a mother's love and the importance of standing for what is right, even in the face of unimaginable grief. Her actions remind me that love doesn't stop, even in the face of loss. I imagine her sitting there day after day, tired and heartbroken but refusing to give up. It's a picture of strength and vulnerability, qualities we all have but sometimes struggle to embrace.

She teaches us that love, persistence, and a commitment to justice can create ripples that lead to change. Her courage inspires us to stand firm, even in the most challenging circumstances, knowing that our actions can make a lasting impact, no matter how small they seem. Rizpah didn't let her lack of status or resources stop her; she acted out of love and conviction. Let her story and her strength inspire us to keep going, even when the results aren't immediate.

Reflections on Love and Loyalty

As we close this chapter on love and loyalty, we reflect on the power of these virtues to transform lives and communities.

Love is often tested by pride, disappointment, or understanding and requires healing. This may mean humbling ourselves, asking forgiveness, or granting grace. God's love empowers us to remain loyal, even when circumstances feel uncertain or challenging.

Through Ruth's unwavering commitment, Hannah's faithful prayers, Michal's complex love, Abigail's peacemaking wisdom, and Rizpah's courageous vigil, we see that love and loyalty transcend time, culture, and circumstance. Their experiences remind us that love isn't always easy and loyalty often demands sacrifice. They inspire us to be better, to love more deeply, and to act with intention. Let us carry these lessons forward, allowing them to shape our relationships and those around us.

4

MOTHERS OF FAITH

4.1 LEAH AND RACHEL: SIBLING RIVALRY AND LOVE

L eah and Rachel were sisters embroiled in a rivalry that might put even the most dramatic soap opera to shame. Their story takes place in the ancient land of Haran, where love, jealousy, and the quest for recognition swirl together like ingredients in a particularly spicy stew.

Jacob fell in love with Rachel, the younger and more beautiful of the sisters. Already sounds like the beginning of a childhood fairytale doesn't it? He worked seven years to marry her, but on their wedding night, Laban deceived Jacob by giving him Leah, the older sister, instead. Jacob later married Rachel, but this set the stage for a lifetime of tension between the sisters. This chain of events sets the stage for complicated and painful family dynamics.

> *Now Laban had two daughters; the name of the older*
> *was Leah, and the name of the younger was Rachel.*
> *Leah had weak eyes, but Rachel had a lovely figure*
> *and was beautiful. Jacob was in love with Rachel*

and said, "I'll work for you seven years in return for your younger daughter Rachel." Laban said, "It's better that I give her to you than to some other man. Stay here with me." So Jacob served seven years to get Rachel, but they seemed like only a few days to him because of his love for her.

Then Jacob said to Laban, "Give me my wife. My time is completed, and I want to make love to her." So Laban brought together all the people of the place and gave a feast. But when evening came, he took his daughter Leah and brought her to Jacob, and Jacob made love to her. And Laban gave his servant Zilpah to his daughter as her attendant.

When morning came, there was Leah! So Jacob said to Laban, "What is this you have done to me? I served you for Rachel, didn't I? Why have you deceived me?" Laban replied, "It is not our custom here to give the younger daughter in marriage before the older one. Finish this daughter's bridal week; then we will give you the younger one also, in return for another seven years of work."

And Jacob did so. He finished the week with Leah, and then Laban gave him his daughter Rachel to be his wife. Laban gave his servant Bilhah to his daughter Rachel as her attendant. Jacob made love to Rachel also, and his love for Rachel was greater than his love for Leah. And he worked for Laban another seven years.

— GENESIS 29:16-30 NIV

While Rachel's beauty captivated Jacob, Leah's marriage to him was marked by her longing for love that often seemed just out of reach. Jacob's favoritism profoundly influenced the dynamics between the two sisters. This rivalry wasn't just about who sat next to Jacob at dinner. It was a constant struggle for his love and affirmation. This rivalry simmered beneath the surface of every family gathering, weaving tension into their lives. Leah named her children with meanings that expressed her deep yearning for Jacob's love, while Rachel's focus was often on motherhood. Their rivalry is defined by Leah's desire for love and Rachel's desire to fulfill the role of a mother.

Leah and Rachel's relationship was complicated by their shared husband, Jacob, whose heart leaned noticeably toward Rachel. With her undeniable beauty and Jacob's affection, Rachel seemed to have everything Leah longed for. This familial drama wasn't just personal—it laid the foundation for the future tribes of Israel, reminding us that even in the messiest of relationships, there can be divine purpose.

Despite the rivalry, Leah and Rachel's legacy as mothers is profound. Leah, the less favored wife, bore Jacob six sons, including Judah and Levi, whose descendants would play critical roles in Israel's history. Judah's lineage would eventually lead to King David and, ultimately, Jesus Christ. Levi's descendants became the priestly tribe entrusted with spiritual leadership. Leah's story is a testament to how God often works through unexpected means, using those who feel overlooked to fulfill His purposes. Leah felt unloved, but God's compassion for her was evident in how He blessed her with children. We are reminded that even when people overlook us, God never does.

When the Lord saw that Leah was not loved, he enabled her to conceive, but Rachel remained childless.

— GENESIS 29:31 NIV

Meanwhile, Rachel, though she struggled with infertility and the deep frustration it brought, ultimately became the mother of Joseph and Benjamin. Joseph, with his dreams and Technicolor coat, would rise to prominence in Egypt, saving his family during a time of famine. Rachel's eventual motherhood was seen as a removal of disgrace, highlighting God's faithfulness in her story.

Their stories teach us about resilience in the face of personal challenges. Although Leah felt unloved by her husband, her faith in God remained constant. Her faith reminds us that our worth isn't defined by human affection but by God's unwavering love. Rachel's struggles with infertility and her eventual triumph illustrate the tension many women feel between societal expectations and personal desires.

Rachel's envy of Leah and Leah's longing for Jacob's love highlight the dangers of comparing ourselves to others. Both women teach us that resilience is not just about enduring hardship but trusting that God's plan is unfolding in ways we may not immediately see. Their lives offer lessons in faith, teaching us to hold onto hope even when the path is fraught with challenges.

In today's world, sibling rivalry, much like Leah and Rachel's, can manifest in subtle ways—whether it's who got the bigger slice of cake or who's mom's favorite (though we all know moms don't have favorites, right?). Managing such rivalry requires intention and grace. Promoting harmony and understanding among siblings involves encouraging open communication and celebrating each other's unique strengths. It's about fostering an environment where differences are appreciated, and love is unconditional. Encouraging mutual support and love despite differences helps build a foundation of trust and unity that can weather life's storms. Learning from Leah and

Rachel's complex relationship can create family dynamics that reflect love, understanding, and resilience.

Deeper Insight

Take a moment to reflect on the dynamics in your family. Are there areas where you see echoes of Leah and Rachel's rivalry? How might Leah and Rachel's story challenge you to seek reconciliation and understanding in relationships strained by jealousy or competition? Have you ever struggled to see your blessings because you were focused on what others have? What steps can you take to cultivate gratitude and contentment in your life? What can Leah's story teach us about finding our identity and worth in God rather than in the approval of others? In what ways has God shown His faithfulness to you, even in difficult or disappointing circumstances?

Final Thoughts

Who hasn't felt overlooked like Leah or compared themselves to someone else like Rachel? Their struggles feel so ordinary, yet their story shows us that God is always working, even amid our imperfections. Leah's journey to finding joy in God's love inspires me to look beyond earthly validation, while Rachel's eventual blessing reminds me to trust in God's faithfulness, even in seasons of waiting.

Leah and Rachel's story reminds us that life isn't always fair, relationships aren't always easy, and people aren't perfect. But God's love is constant, His plans are good, and His purposes are more significant than our struggles. Their lives encourage us to trust Him, even when life feels tangled.

Jochebed was a Hebrew woman from the tribe of Levi. She was a mother in ancient Egypt, living under the oppressive rule of Pharaoh, who had ordered the death of every newborn Hebrew boy. It was a time of unimaginable fear, yet Jochebed's heart was filled with an unyielding resolve. She made bold and faithful decisions to protect her child, Moses, trusting God's plan even when the path ahead was uncertain.

Jochebed, meaning "Yahweh is glory," embodies her name by her deep faith and strength. She and her husband, Amram, were part of the Levite tribe, a lineage destined for spiritual leadership. Jochebed was the mother of three remarkable children - Miriam, Aaron, and Moses - each of whom played significant roles in the story of Israel's liberation. When Moses was born, Jochebed saw that he was a special child, and she couldn't bear to see him perish. With the tenacity that only a mother knows, she hid him for three months, risking her own life in defiance of Pharaoh's cruel edict.

Jochebed's ingenuity came to the fore when hiding Moses was no longer an option. She crafted a small basket, waterproofed it with tar and pitch, and placed baby Moses inside. Then, with a heart full of fear and hope, she set the basket afloat on the Nile River. This was no casual decision; it was an act of profound trust in God's plan for her child.

> *Now a man of the tribe of Levi married a Levite*
> *woman, and she became pregnant and gave birth to*
> *a son. When she saw that he was a fine child, she*
> *hid him for three months. But when she could hide*
> *him no longer, she got a papyrus basket for him and*
> *coated it with tar and pitch. Then she placed the*
> *child in it and put it among the reeds along the bank*

*of the Nile. His sister stood at a distance to see what
would happen to him.*

— EXODUS 2:1-4 NIV

As she watched the basket drift away, she entrusted her daughter, Miriam, to keep a watchful eye on her brother. Imagine the courage needed to release her son into the unknown and involve her daughter in this dangerous plan. Jochebed's faith was not passive but an active commitment to a divine vision for Moses' life.

Through divine intervention, Pharaoh's daughter discovered the baby and took pity on him. Miriam, Moses' sister, suggested a Hebrew woman to nurse the child—and that woman was Jochebed. Not only was her son's life spared, but Jochebed also had the chance to nurture him during his early years, instilling his faith and identity before he was raised in Pharaoh's household.

> *Then Pharaoh's daughter went down to the Nile to
> bathe, and her attendants were walking along the
> riverbank. She saw the basket among the reeds
> and sent her female slave to get it. She opened it
> and saw the baby. He was crying, and she felt
> sorry for him. "This is one of the Hebrew babies,"
> she said.*
> *Then his sister asked Pharaoh's daughter, "Shall I go
> and get one of the Hebrew women to nurse the baby
> for you?" "Yes, go," she answered. So the girl went
> and got the baby's mother. Pharaoh's daughter said
> to her, "Take this baby and nurse him for me, and I
> will pay you." So the woman took the baby and
> nursed him. When the child grew older, she took
> him to Pharaoh's daughter and he became her son.*

She named him Moses, saying, "I drew him out of the water."

— EXODUS 2:5-10 NIV

Jochebed's faith was characterized by her ability to see beyond the immediate danger. Her faith guided her through the oppression, giving her the courage to defy Pharaoh's orders. She trusted that God had a plan for Moses, a plan that was far greater than the threats of any earthly ruler.

Her actions were protective and prophetic, laying the groundwork for Moses' future as a leader. In placing Moses in the Nile, Jochebed was not merely letting go; she put him directly into God's hands, trusting that His purpose would prevail. Her faith was a declaration of hope in the face of despair, a testament to the power of divine providence.

The impact of Jochebed's courageous decisions is seen in Moses' life and leadership. Raised initially by Jochebed herself, Moses was imbued with a strong sense of identity and faith. Jochebed raised Moses thanks to Pharaoh's daughter, who had unknowingly hired her as his nurse. Jochebed's teachings influenced Moses' understanding of God, shaping his character and convictions. These early years, spent under his mother's care, were pivotal in forming the foundation of Moses' leadership and spiritual journey. Jochebed's influence was instrumental in preparing Moses to lead the Israelites out of Egypt. Her legacy lives on in the story of a man who would stand before Pharaoh and declare, "Let my people go."

In today's world, Jochebed's courage offers valuable lessons for us as parents and guardians. Encouraging faith-driven decision-making in challenging times means trusting the bigger picture, even when the immediate future looks bleak. Jochebed's story teaches us the importance of nurturing spiritual values in our children, instilling in them the strength and faith to face whatever challenges life might bring. Her story also encourages us to partner with God in raising children who understand their worth and purpose. Her life reminds us that courage is not the absence of fear but the determination to act despite it, trusting in God's plan for the lives of those we love most.

Deeper Insight

Reflect on a time when you faced a situation where you needed to trust God despite fear or uncertainty. Are there areas in your life where you need to let go and trust God with someone or something you hold dear? What can you do to learn to trust God in difficult or frightening circumstances? Are there areas where you need to surrender control and trust God's plan? What role does faith play in shaping the lives of those we influence as parents, mentors, or friends? What role does faith play in shaping your own life? Jochebed didn't know what would happen to Moses but acted in faith anyway. What small steps of faith can you take in your current situation?

Final Thoughts

Jochebed's story deeply resonates with me because it's about trusting God when everything feels out of control. Placing Moses in the basket wasn't an act of giving up; it was an act of surrender, trusting that God would guide and protect him. Her story demonstrates how God works through the courage and faith of ordinary people to accomplish extraordinary things. Her life encourages us to trust God with the things that matter most and act courageously, knowing He can bring hope and redemption in even the darkest moments.

Thinking about her courage inspires me to let go of the things I try to control and trust that God's plans are greater than mine. God often works in ways we don't expect, bringing blessings and opportunities we could never orchestrate alone.

Imagine a bustling temple courtyard filled with the sound of coins clinking as wealthy patrons make ostentatious donations. In this lively scene, a humble widow quietly approaches the offering box. With trembling hands, she drops two small copper coins worth only a fraction of a penny into the box. To the casual observer, her contribution is negligible, quickly overshadowed by the grand offerings surrounding her.

However, Jesus noticed. His keen eyes saw the monetary value and the heart behind the gift. In this moment, He called His disciples together, pointing out the widow's act as an extraordinary expression of faith.

> *"Truly, I tell you," He said, "this poor widow has more into the treasury than all the others. They all gave out of their wealth; but she, out of her poverty, put in everything-all she had to live on."*

> — MARK 12:43-44 NIV

Her offering, small in the world's eyes, was monumental in the eyes of God, for it represented everything she had.

The widow's act starkly contrasted with the offerings of the wealthy, who gave from their abundance without any real sacrifice. Their contributions, though large in number, lacked the depth of commitment that the widow's two coins embodied. She gave all she had, entrusting her entire livelihood to God. This selfless act of giving was a profound display of trust and surrender, a testament to her belief that God would provide.

Her faith was not contingent on material wealth but on the assurance that God was her provider. In a society that often equates wealth with success, the widow's offering challenges us to redefine generosity. It's not about the size of the gift but the spirit in which it is given. Her story reminds us that true generosity involves sacrifice, a willingness to give until it costs us something.

In Jesus' teachings, the widow's offering is a powerful illustration of the heart of giving. It's not about the amount but the intent. The widow's coins, though small, held immense value in God's kingdom because they came from a heart of complete devotion and trust. This story teaches us to look beyond the surface and value the sincerity behind our actions. It's a lesson that resonates deeply, urging us to examine our motives. Are we giving out of abundance, or are we willing to step into sacrificial generosity? The widow's example invites us to consider what it means to give all, challenging us to live with open hands and trusting hearts.

In today's world, practicing selfless generosity can be transformative. It's not just about financial giving; it's about offering our time, talents, and resources for the benefit of others. We are encouraged to trust in God's provision, knowing that when we give from a place of love and faith, our contributions, however small, can have a profound impact.

Whether volunteering at a local shelter, supporting a friend in need, or contributing to a cause close to your heart, acts of generosity can ripple out to touch lives in ways we might never fully see. The widow's story inspires us to embrace a giving spirit that reflects God's love and grace in a desperately needy world.

Deeper Insight

God doesn't measure our gifts by their size but by the spirit in which they are given. The widow's offering was small in monetary value but enormous in faith and love. Have you ever given more than you can afford, trusting that God will see you through? Have you ever given and realized later you received so much more than you contributed? What steps can you take to deepen your faith in God's care and provision? How does this story encourage you to give from love and faith rather than obligation or recognition?

Final Thoughts

The story of the widow's mite is especially touching because it challenges me to think about the true value of my contributions —big and small. There have been times when I've hesitated to give because I felt my resources were too limited, yet I'm reminded that God isn't impressed by the size of our gift but by the heart that gives. The widow's mite teaches us that no act of faith is too small for God to notice. The widow's example pushes me to trust that even when I feel like I have nothing to offer, I can still make a difference when I give with a sincere heart. I have found that when I trust in God and give even when I think I can't, my gift is returned to me in abundance.

Her story inspires us to trust, give, and live with open hands, knowing that God will honor our efforts when they come from a place of love and faith. Additionally, the widow didn't make a scene or draw attention to herself. She gave, trusting God to do the rest. Her humility and faithfulness are a powerful example for all of us.

The widow's mite teaches us that every gift matters when it comes from a heart fully surrendered to God. Her story is a gentle, powerful reminder that even small acts of faith can profoundly impact our lives and the world around us. Let her example inspire you to embrace sacrificial giving and to trust that God sees, honors, and multiplies your faithfulness, no matter how small it may seem.

4.4 MARY, MOTHER OF JESUS: FAITH AND FAVOR

Mary was a humble girl from Nazareth, chosen for a divine purpose that would leave most of us speechless. She was a young woman, her heart no doubt full of hopes and dreams, suddenly visited by an angel with news that would forever alter the course of history. Somehow, in the face of the angel Gabriel's announcement, Mary's response was a declaration of faith that echoes through the ages: "Be it unto me according to thy word."

> ...God sent the angel Gabriel to Nazareth, a town in
> Galilee, to a virgin pledged to be married to a man
> named Joseph, a descendant of David. The virgin's
> name was Mary. The angel went to her and said,
> "Greeting, you who are highly favored! The Lord is
> with you." Mary was greatly troubled at his words
> and wondered what kind of greeting this might be.
> But the angel said to her, "Do not be afraid, Mary;
> you have found favor with God. You will conceive
> and give birth to a son, and you are to call him
> Jesus. He will be great and will be called the Son of
> the Most High. The Lord God will give him the
> throne of his father David, and he will reign over
> Jacob's descendants forever; his kingdom will never
> end."
> "How will this be," Mary asked the angel, "since I am a
> virgin?" The angel answered, "The Holy Spirit will
> come on you, and the power of the Most High will
> overshadow you. So the holy one to be born will be
> called the Son of God. Even Elizabeth, your relative
> is going to have a child in her old age, and she who
> was said to be unable to conceive is in her sixth
> month. For no word from God will ever fail." "I am

the Lord's servant, Mary answered. *"May your word to me be fulfilled."*

— LUKE 1:26-38 NIV

As told in Luke 1, the Annunciation was more than a celestial visit; it was when Mary embraced God's plan with a heart full of trust and submission. Her words were not just acceptance but a testament to her understanding of God's sovereignty. Later, in her Magnificat, Mary sang a hymn of praise that revealed her deep faith and comprehension of the divine narrative unfolding before her. Her song wasn't just a melody but a proclamation of joy and reverence, a window into her soul.

Mary's role as the mother of Jesus came with its challenges. Society's whispers must have followed her everywhere, questioning her integrity and Joseph's decision to stand by her. Yet, Joseph, her betrothed, proved to be a steadfast partner, guided by his own angelic dream to protect and love Mary and her unborn child. Together, they navigated the complexities of societal expectations and familial pressures, forging a path of faith and courage.

Their journey to Bethlehem while Mary was heavy with child was a testament to their resilience and trust in God's plan. Imagine the discomfort and uncertainty of finding no room at the inn, yet knowing that the birth of this child was the fulfillment of divine prophecy. In these moments, Mary's strength and grace reveal a profound inner resolve, an unwavering belief in the purpose she was called to fulfill and her trust in God to provide.

Throughout Jesus' life and ministry, Mary's influence and presence were quietly steadfast. At the wedding in Cana, her gentle nudge prompted Jesus' first miracle, turning water into wine, a testament to her belief in His divine mission.

On the third day a wedding took place at Cana in
    Galilee. Jesus' mother was there, and Jesus and his
    disciples had also been invited to the wedding. When
    the wine was gone, Jesus's mother said to him "They
    have no more wine." "Woman, why do you involve
    me?" Jesus replied. "My hour has not yet come." His
    mother said to the servants, "Do whatever he tells
    you."
Nearby stood six stone water jars, the kind used by the
    Jews for ceremonial washing, each holding from
    twenty to thirty gallons. Jesus said to the servants,
    "Fill the jars with water"; so they fill them to the
    brim. Then he told them, "Now draw some out and
    take it to the master of the banquet." They did so,
    and the master of the banquet tasted the water that
    had been turned into wine. He did not realize where
    it had come from, though the servants who had
    drawn the water knew.
Then he called the bridegroom aside and said,
    "Everyone brings out the choice wine first and then
    the cheaper wine after the guests had had too much
    to drink; but you have saved the best till now." What
    Jesus did here in Cana of Galilee with the first of
    the signs through which he revealed his glory, and
    his disciples believed in him.

— JOHN 2:1-11 NIV

As she watched her son's ministry unfold, Mary faced both joy and heartache, witnessing the miracles and teachings that transformed countless lives while bearing the brunt of criticism and disbelief. Her heart must have ached as she stood at the foot of the cross, watching her beloved son suffer and die. Yet, even in this, Mary remained a pillar of strength and faith. Mary's presence at the crucifixion and later at the tomb and her prayer with the apostles after Jesus' ascension all highlight her unwavering commitment to the mission she had accepted so many years before. Mary's life was a tapestry of strength and grace, woven with threads of faith, love, and sacrifice.

> *Near the cross of Jesus stood his mother, his mother's sister, Mary the wife of Clopas, and Mary Magdalene. When Jesus saw his mother there, and the disciple whom he loved standing nearby, he said to her, "Woman, here is your son," and to the disciple, "here is your mother." From that time on, this disciple took her into his home.*
>
> — JOHN 19:25-27 NIV

> *Then the apostles returned to Jerusalem from the hill called the Mount of Olives, a Sabbath day's walk from the city. They all joined together constantly in prayer, along with the women and Mary the mother of Jesus, and with his brothers.*
>
> — ACTS 1:12,14 NIV

In our own lives, Mary's story challenges us to embrace divine purpose with the same faith and grace. Trusting in divine guidance means opening our hearts to the unexpected and welcoming challenges as opportunities for growth. As mothers, mentors, or guides, we are called to nurture faith and purpose in those entrusted to us, supporting them in their journeys of discovery. Mary's faith didn't falter even in the darkest moments. Her faith in God's plan and her example teach us to hold fast to our beliefs, to trust in the unseen, and to find peace in the knowledge that we are part of a story much more signifi-cant than ourselves. Her life is a beacon of hope, a reminder that divine favor often comes clothed in humility and service, guiding us to walk with faith and courage in the paths laid before us.

Deeper Insight

Consider Mary's deep trust in God and His plan. She endured immense challenges as the mother of Jesus. How can her example encourage you in seasons of struggle? Does her example inspire you to stand firm in love and faith during diffi-cult times? What role does your faith play in helping you perse-vere through life's challenges? What moments or blessings can you remember to treasure and thank God for today? What does Mary's example teach us about the lasting impact of love, faith, and presence in the lives of those we care for? What does Mary's presence at the cross teach us about showing up for others, even when difficult? Mary stood by Jesus even when hope seemed lost. How can we demonstrate such steadfast faith in our own lives?

Final Thoughts

The story of Mary's journey always amazes and humbles me. Sometimes, when I feel overwhelmed by the unknown or burdened by life's challenges, I'm reminded of how Mary trusted God's plan even when she couldn't see it fully. Can you imagine, young and unsure of the world, being visited by angels and told you'll be the mother of the Son of God? Her example teaches me that it's okay to be vulnerable, to lean into God's promises, and to find strength in the quiet moments of prayer and reflection. Sometimes, it's difficult to balance the busyness of life with the need for spiritual quiet. Mary's story gently encourages us to prioritize that time with God.

Mary, the mother of Jesus, exemplifies the power of a humble heart open to God's call. Her life is a tapestry of unexpected challenges and divine grace—a reminder that God is at work every season, whether in joy or sorrow. Let her story inspire us to trust in God's greater plan, embrace humility, and find solace in the quiet, transformative moments of faith.

4.5 ELIZABETH: JOY AND EXPECTATION

Elizabeth was *a descendant of Aaron* (**Luke 1:5 NIV**), the first high priest of Israel. Her lineage means she came from a long line of priests and religious leaders. This was a significant heritage in Jewish culture, as the priestly line was set apart for serving God in the Temple. She was also related to Mary, the mother of Jesus, possibly a cousin or aunt.

Elizabeth was the wife of Zechariah, a priest. Together, they were a holy couple dedicated to God's service. Together, they represented faithfulness, righteousness, and devotion to God's law. Although she was a faithful and devoted servant of God, she spent many years shrouded in the whispers of barrenness. She was childless during a time when not having children was often seen as a mark of disgrace. Even so, Elizabeth remained faithful, her heart steadfast in prayer.

One day, while Zechariah was serving in the temple, the angel Gabriel appeared before him. The angel delivered astounding news: Elizabeth would bear a son, and he would be great in the eyes of the Lord.

> *Then an angel of the Lord appeared to him, standing at
> the right side of the altar of incense. When
> Zechariah saw him, he was startled and was
> gripped with fear. But the angel said to him: "Do
> not be afraid, Zechariah; your prayer has been
> heard. Your wife Elizabeth will bear you a son, and
> you are to call him John. He will be a joy and
> delight to you, and many will rejoice because of his
> birth, for he will be great in the sight of the Lord.
> He is never to take wine or other fermented drink,
> and he will be filled with the Holy Spirit even
> before he is born. He will bring back many of the*

people of Israel to the Lord their God. And he will
go on before the Lord, in the spirit and power of
Elijah, to turn the hearts of the parents to their
children and the disobedient to the wisdom of the
righteous—to make ready a people prepared for the
Lord."

Zechariah asked the angel, "How can I be sure of this? I
am an old man and my wife is well along in years."
The angel said to him, "I am Gabriel. I stand in the
presence of God, and I have been sent to speak to
you and to tell you this good news. And now you
will be silent and not able to speak until the day this
happens, because you did not believe my words,
which will come true at their appointed time."

— LUKE 1:11-20 NIV

Zechariah was astonished and questioned the angel, stating that he and Elizabeth were beyond childbearing years. The angel struck him mute for doubting until the birth came to pass.

When his time of service was completed, he returned
home. After this his wife Elizabeth became pregnant
and for five months remained in seclusion. "The
Lord has done this for me," she said. "In these days
he has shown his favor and taken away my disgrace
among the people."

— LUKE 1:23-25 NIV

Elizabeth embraced the news of her pregnancy with faith and gratitude. The waiting had been long, but her faith never wavered. Elizabeth's pregnancy was a testament to her resilience and God's perfect timing.

The encounter between Mary and Elizabeth is one of those rare moments in scripture where you can almost feel the joy leap off the page. Mary came to visit Elizabeth after the angel Gabriel visited her. Gabriel told Mary about Elizabeth's pregnancy; remember, Elizabeth had waited many years to have a child, and this would have been known by her family.

When Mary, newly pregnant with Jesus, visits Elizabeth, it's a meeting of miracles. As Mary greets her, Elizabeth feels the baby—John the Baptist—move in her womb.

> *At that time Mary got ready and hurried to a town in the hill country of Judea, where she entered Zechariah's home and greeted Elizabeth. When Elizabeth heard Mary's greeting, the baby leaped in her womb, and Elizabeth was filled with the Holy Spirit.*
>
> *In a loud voice she exclaimed: "Blessed are you among women, and blessed is the child you will bear! But why am I so favored, that the mother of my Lord should come to me? As soon as the sound of your greeting reached my ears, the baby in my womb leaped for joy. Blessed is she who has believed that the Lord would fulfill his promises to her!"*
>
> — LUKE 1:39-45 NIV

Imagine the joy and expectation that filled the room, two women bonded by divine intervention, each carrying a child destined to change the world. Elizabeth's recognition of Mary's child as her Lord is profound. She doesn't question or doubt; she knows. Her words, filled with the Holy Spirit, confirm Mary's divine purpose and ignite a song of praise that echoes through both their lives. Mary's response to Elizabeth's recognition is known as Mary's Song or Mary's Magnificat.

Mary's Magnificat (Luke 1:46-55 NIV)

And Mary said: "My soul glorifies the Lord and my
spirit rejoices in God my Savior, for he has been
mindful of the humble state of his servant.

From now on all generations will call me blessed, for the
Mighty One has done great things for me—holy is
his name.

His mercy extends to those who fear him, from genera-
tion to generation.

He has performed mighty deeds with his arm; he has
scattered those who are proud in their inmost
thoughts.

He has brought down rulers from their thrones but has
lifted up the humble.

He has filled the hungry with good things but has sent
the rich away empty.

He has helped his servant Israel, remembering to be
merciful to Abraham and his descendants forever,
just as he promised our ancestors

— LUKE 1:46-55 NIV

Elizabeth was one of the first to recognize Jesus as the Messiah. She also played a crucial role in affirming Mary's faith. God placed these two women together to encourage and support each other during their unexpected pregnancies.

Elizabeth's role in John's life began long before he was born. Her son, John the Baptist, wasn't just any child but one of the greatest prophets in history. Her influence on his upbringing is evident in the strength of his prophetic mission. You can picture her gently guiding him, instilling faith and purpose.

When it was time for Elizabeth to have her baby, she

*gave birth to a son. Her neighbors and relatives
heard that the Lord had shown her great mercy, and
they shared her joy.*

*On the eighth day they came to circumcise the child,
and they were going to name him after his father
Zechariah, but his mother spoke up and said, "No!
He is to be called John."*

*They said to her, "There is no one among your relatives
who has that name."*

*Then they made signs to his father, to find out what he
would like to name the child. He asked for a writing
tablet, and to everyone's astonishment he wrote,
"His name is John." Immediately his mouth was
opened and his tongue set free, and he began to
speak, praising God. All the neighbors were filled
with awe, and throughout the hill country of Judea
people were talking about all these things. Everyone
who heard this wondered about it, asking, "What
then is this child going to be?" For the Lord's hand
was with him.*

— LUKE 1:57-66 NIV

The birth of John was not just a redeeming victory for Elizabeth; it was a pivotal moment in God's plan. His naming ceremony, during which Zechariah's speech is restored, marks the beginning of John's public identity and his role as the one who would prepare the way for Jesus. Elizabeth's nurturing presence was instrumental in shaping John's character and spiritual formation, preparing him for the wilderness and the mission that lay ahead.

Theologically, Elizabeth's story is rich and significant. Her recognition of the Messiah's coming places her in the broader narrative of salvation. She stands as a bridge between the old and new covenants, and her life is a testimony to God's faithfulness across generations.

Elizabeth's prophetic role in affirming Mary's calling offers a glimpse into the interconnectedness of God's plans, where every thread is woven together with purpose. Her story invites us to see our lives as part of this divine tapestry, recognizing that we, too, have roles to play in the unfolding story of redemption.

Today, Elizabeth's joy and expectation encourage us to embrace hope and patience while waiting for God's promises to unfold. Her story teaches us the beauty of celebrating and affirming others' callings and recognizing the divine in the mundane. It reminds us that joy isn't just a feeling; it's a choice to trust in something greater than ourselves.

In a world often rushing toward the next big thing, Elizabeth's life calls us to pause, to savor the moments of expectation, and to find joy in the waiting. As we do, we open our hearts to the possibilities of what God can do in our lives, just as He did in hers.

Deeper Insight

Think of a time when you were waiting on some event or news that was important to you. How do you handle waiting, knowing that God's timing might differ from yours? Does Elizabeth's story encourage you to trust God's plan and perfect timing? Does her faith remind you to remain steadfast even when answers to prayers seem far off? Have you ever experienced someone affirming God's work in your life? How did it affect you? Can you intentionally celebrate the blessings and successes of others without comparison or envy? What moments in your life can you look back on as evidence of God's goodness?

Final Thoughts

Elizabeth's story is about patience, faith, and God's perfect timing. For years, Elizabeth longed for a child until God did something miraculous. Even while waiting, she understood that God was working. God's timing is perfect, even when we don't understand it. He hears our prayers and His answers come at the right time. Her life reminds us that delays aren't denials and that God's best gifts sometimes come when we least expect them.

I love Elizabeth's story because it speaks of seasons of waiting—and let's be honest, waiting is hard. Sometimes, I pray for something and hope for an instant answer, but Elizabeth's life reminds me that God's timing is different from mine—and always better. God's delays are not His denials. She teaches us to be faithful in the waiting, joyful in the blessing, and humble in the presence of God's plan.

I'm also struck by her ability to celebrate Mary's blessing without resentment. That's a lesson I need frequently! It's easy to look at others and think, *"God, why them and not me?"* a blessing that can go either way. Elizabeth shows that when we trust God's timing, we can truly rejoice with others without bitterness.

So, if you're waiting on something today, take heart—God is still working. When He does move, it will be worth the wait.

Reflections on Mothers of Faith

As I close this chapter on mothers of faith, I think about these women's profound impact on their families and the world. They faced unique and sometimes monumental challenges: Leah and Rachel with their sibling rivalry, Jochebad hiding her son Moses from Pharaoh, the Widow and her mite of offering trusting in God's providence, Mary the mother of Jesus and her surrender to God's will, and Elizabeth patiently waiting on God's timing for a child.

Reflecting on their stories, I ask myself, do I trust that God is still working for my good? Am I focused on things I lack rather than the blessings I have been given? Is my faith strong enough to endure even when I don't understand my role in God's plan? Do I have the patience and faith to recognize that His timing might differ from mine?

Faith isn't about having a perfect life or having perfect solutions to challenges that occur. Faith is about trusting in God. Their stories encourage us to release our fears and trust God's plan and provision. They remind us that God honors the smallest acts of faith and fulfills His promises in His appointed time. God is always present, working, and faithful, whether we are waiting, surrendering, giving, or seeking our worth. Always.

WISDOM AND UNDERSTANDING

5.1 QUEEN OF SHEBA: SEEKING WISDOM

Once upon a time, in a land rich with spice-laden winds and sun-baked sands, there lived a woman whose wisdom was said to rival the very stars in the sky. She was known as the Queen of Sheba, a woman of legendary intellect and curiosity, a woman whose story reminds us that the pursuit of wisdom is timeless and universal.

She was a powerful and wealthy queen who could have sat comfortably in her opulent palace, sipping on the finest teas and enjoying the adoration of her subjects. But this queen had a thirst for knowledge that couldn't be quenched by mere luxury. She had heard tales of a king whose wisdom was said to surpass all others—King Solomon of Israel. Intrigued and determined, she embarked on a journey that would become a tale of wisdom-seeking grandeur.

The Queen of Sheba's quest for knowledge was no small endeavor. She prepared meticulously, gathering an entourage fit for... well, a queen. Her caravan was loaded with gifts that would tempt any king: gold, precious stones, and the finest spices. These were tokens of her wealth and symbols of her respect for Solomon's reputation.

Her journey from the ancient kingdom of Sheba, believed to be part of present-day Yemen, to the land of Israel was long and arduous. This long trek spoke volumes about her determination. As she traveled, the queen must have pondered the questions she would ask Solomon, each inquiry a test of his legendary wisdom. Her arrival in Jerusalem was not only a meeting of royalty but a confluence of cultures. This event would resonate throughout history.

When the Queen of Sheba finally stood before Solomon, she was not there to flatter or to be flattered. She came armed with questions that would challenge even the wisest of minds. These were not riddles for amusement but inquiries that delved into the depths of understanding and governance.

> She came to Solomon and talked with him about all that she had on her mind. Solomon answered all her questions; nothing was too hard for the king to explain to her. When the queen of Sheba saw all the wisdom of Solomon and the palace he had built, the food on his table, the seating of his officials, the attending servants in their robes, his cupbearers, and the burnt offerings he made at the temple of the Lord, she was overwhelmed.
>
> She said to the king, "The report I heard in my own country about your achievements and your wisdom is true. But I did not believe these things until I came and saw with my own eyes. Indeed, not even half was told me; in wisdom and wealth you have far exceeded the report I heard. How happy your people must be! How happy your officials, who

continually stand before you and hear your wisdom!
Praise be to the Lord your God, who has delighted in
you and placed you on the throne of Israel. Because
of the Lord's eternal love for Israel, he has made you
king to maintain justice and righteousness."

— 1 KINGS 10:2-9 NIV

Solomon answered them all with his God-given wisdom, leaving the queen astounded. Her response was one of admiration and acknowledgment. She saw not only the wealth of his kingdom but the divine favor that rested upon him. The gifts they exchanged were more than mere pleasantries; they were expressions of mutual respect and recognition of each other's greatness. The Queen of Sheba's declaration of Solomon's divine favor was a testament to her commitment to discovering truth through dialogue and learning.

The cultural and diplomatic impact of her visit was immense. The meeting of these two great minds forged a bond between their kingdoms, establishing diplomatic and trade relations that would benefit both Israel and Sheba. The exchange of goods and ideas was not just an economic boon but a cultural enrichment. The exchange blended traditions and innovations that would influence both societies. This meeting strengthened political and cultural ties, paving the way for future interactions between nations. It was a reminder that wisdom and understanding can bridge divides, creating connections that transcend borders.

The Queen of Sheba's curiosity offers valuable lessons in our modern world. Her journey teaches us the importance of pursuing truth with curiosity and integrity. She reminds us that wisdom is not something to be passively received but actively sought.

Her story encourages us to embrace open-mindedness and pursue knowledge with a spirit of inquiry. In doing so, we open ourselves to the richness of understanding that comes from diverse perspectives. The value of intercultural exchanges and relationships is as relevant today as it was in the days of the Queen of Sheba. By seeking wisdom and fostering dialogue, we can create connections that enrich our lives and the world around us.

Deeper Insight

Take a moment to reflect on your own quest for wisdom. What questions are you seeking answers to, and would you pursue them with the same curiosity and integrity as the Queen of Sheba? Consider engaging in a dialogue with someone from a different background or perspective, and note the insights you might gain from this exchange. Are you willing to set aside pride and admit when you can learn from someone else, even when the source is unexpected? Does the Queen of Sheba's exchange with Solomon inspire you to seek meaningful, collaborative relationships? How would you cultivate a heart that rejoices in others' blessings?

Final Thoughts

I find Queen of Sheba's story incredibly inspiring because it challenges me to look beyond surface-level beauty and wealth and, instead, to pursue a deeper understanding of truth. Her journey reminds me that sometimes, the most significant transformations in our lives come when we are willing to ask tough questions and seek genuine answers. I'm encouraged by her example of stepping out in faith—even as a ruler—showing that no matter our status, we're all invited to explore God's wisdom.

Her story also prompts me to examine my own heart: am I willing to be curious and humble enough to learn, and do I celebrate the talents and blessings in others as reflections of God's love? It's a reminder that true wisdom is shared generously and that every act of sincere inquiry can open the door to a deeper, more meaningful relationship with God. Her recognition of God's role in Solomon's success also challenges me to consider how I acknowledge God's blessings in my life.

The Queen of Sheba's journey is a testament to the transformative power of curiosity, humility, and generosity. Her example invites us to seek truth boldly, approach life with an open heart, and honor the ways God works through both the extraordinary and the everyday. I hope her story encourages you to ask the questions that lead to deeper faith, give generously from what you have, and recognize the divine spark in every encounter.

5.2 THE SHUNAMMITE WOMAN: FAITH AND HOSPITALITY

In a quiet village nestled in the hills of ancient Israel, there lived a woman whose name we never learn but whose actions speak volumes. The Shunammite woman, as she is known, was a figure of profound generosity and faith. She was a wealthy, influential woman who lived in, as you might have guessed, the town of Shunem.

Her story, found in the Second Book of Kings, begins with an act of hospitality that would ripple through her life in ways she never could have anticipated. It all started when she noticed the prophet Elisha passing through her village regularly.

Rather than just offering him a meal, she decided to go even further. She and her husband built a small room on their roof, a sanctuary for Elisha to rest whenever he traveled their way. This room, furnished with a bed, a table, a chair, and a lamp, symbolized her open heart and willingness to serve. This act of generosity and thoughtfulness reflects her deep care for others and her recognition of Elisha as a man of God.

> *One day Elisha went to Shunem. And a well-to-do woman was there, who urged him to stay for a meal. So whenever he came by, he stopped there to eat. She said to her husband, "I know that this man who often comes our way is a holy man of God. Let's make a small room on the roof and put in it a bed and a table, a chair and a lamp for him. Then he can stay there whenever he comes to us."*
>
> — 2 KINGS 4:8-10 NIV

Her hospitality didn't stop there. The Shunammite woman's care for Elisha went beyond providing a place to stay. She offered ongoing support, ensuring he had what he needed during his visits. Her support wasn't just about meeting the physical needs of a weary traveler; it was an expression of deep respect for Elisha's prophetic mission.

Her initiative in providing this level of care demonstrated a profound understanding of the importance of supporting God's work. It was an act of faith in action, a tangible way to participate in the divine mission unfolding around her. This kind of generosity, rooted in a sincere desire to help, is something we can all aspire to emulate in our own lives.

Elisha was touched by her kindness and wanted to bless her in return. The Shunammite woman humbly declined any reward, saying she had all she needed. However, Elisha, moved by her selflessness, prophesied that the Shunammite woman would have a son despite her husband's old age. Despite her initial doubt, she gave birth to a son the following year.

> One day when Elisha came, he went up to his room and lay down there. He said to his servant Gehazi, "Call the Shunammite." So he called her, and she stood before him. Elisha said to him, "Tell her, 'You have gone to all this trouble for us. Now what can be done for you? Can we speak on your behalf to the king or the commander of the army?'" She replied, "I have a home among my own people."
> "What can be done for her?" Elisha asked.
> Gehazi said, "She has no son, and her husband is old."
> Then Elisha said, "Call her." So he called her, and she stood in the doorway. "About this time next year," Elisha said, "you will hold a son in your arms."

> *"No, my lord!" she objected. "Please, man of God, don't*
> *mislead your servant!"*
> *But the woman became pregnant, and the next year*
> *about that same time she gave birth to a son, just as*
> *Elisha had told her.*

— 2 KINGS 4:11-17 NIV

But life, as we know, isn't always so straightforward. The Shunammite woman's faith was soon tested in a way she never expected. Despite her kindness and generosity, she faced the heart-wrenching tragedy of losing her young son. Imagine the depth of her grief, the sense of loss that must have enveloped her.

Even in the face of this personal tragedy, she exhibited unwavering faith. Rather than succumbing to despair, she laid her son on the prophet's bed and set out to find Elisha. Her journey was not one of despair but of hope. She believed, even amid her sorrow, that God's power could restore her son to life. Her decision to seek Elisha's help was a testament to her faith, a refusal to let tragedy have the final word. When she reached Elisha, she clung to him and expressed her grief. Still, her actions demonstrated her unshakable belief that God could restore her son's life.

Elisha, moved by her faith and determination, returned with her to her home. The miracle of restoration that followed was nothing short of extraordinary. There, he performed an act that would revive her son. This miracle underscored the power of faith in the face of insurmountable odds. Elisha's role in this miracle was pivotal, but the Shunammite woman's faith set the stage for what God would do. Her expression of gratitude and faith following this miracle was a testament to her understanding of God's goodness and sovereignty. It was a profound moment of restoration, not just of life but of hope and faith renewed.

> When Elisha reached the house, there was the boy lying
> dead on his couch. He went in, shut the door on the
> two of them and prayed to the Lord. Then he got on
> the bed and lay on the boy, mouth to mouth, eyes to
> eyes, hands to hands. As he stretched himself out on
> him, the boy's body grew warm. Elisha turned
> away and walked back and forth in the room and
> then got on the bed and stretched out on him once
> more. The boy sneezed seven times and opened his
> eyes.
> Elisha summoned Gehazi and said, "Call the Shunam-
> mite." And he did. When she came, he said, "Take
> your son." She came in, fell at his feet and bowed to
> the ground. Then she took her son and went out.

— 2 KINGS 4:32-37 NIV

The story didn't end there. The Shunammite woman's ongoing care for Elisha bore fruit in ways she couldn't have predicted. When a seven-year famine threatened her land, she and her household relocated to the land of the Philistines, heeding Elisha's prophetic warning.

This move, though difficult, was a testament to her continued faith and trust in God's provision. When she returned to Shunem, she found the king had taken over her land. But, as fate would have it, she arrived at the king's court just as Gehazi, Elisha's servant, recounted her earlier miracle. Her appeal to the king for the return of her lands was met with favor, and her property was restored. This act of divine justice was a powerful reminder of the ongoing care by God for those who live by faith and generosity.

At the end of the seven years she came back from the
land of the Philistines and went to appeal to the
king for her house and land. The king was talking
to Gehazi, the servant of the man of God, and had
said, "Tell me about all the great things Elisha has
done." Just as Gehazi was telling the king how
Elisha had restored the dead to life, the woman
whose son Elisha had brought back to life came to
appeal to the king for her house and land.

Gehazi said, "This is the woman, my lord the king, and
this is her son whom Elisha restored to life." The
king asked the woman about it, and she told him.
Then he assigned an official to her case and said to
him, "Give back everything that belonged to her,
including all the income from her land from the day
she left the country until now."

— 2 KINGS 8:3-6 NIV

The Shunammite woman's story offers timeless insights into the power of faith and hospitality. In our modern world, her example encourages us to practice hospitality and service within our communities. It's about more than opening our doors; it's about opening our hearts, offering support where it's needed, and participating in the work of God through acts of kindness.

Her unwavering faith teaches us about conviction and perseverance, showing us that even in the face of personal tragedy, hope is never lost when faith is our guide. Her life reminds us that our actions, rooted in faith and generosity, can have far-reaching effects, touching lives and bringing about change in ways we might never foresee.

As we reflect on the Shunammite woman's legacy, let us find inspiration in her story to live with open hearts and steadfast faith. Her life reminds us that even in our ordinary days, we have the power to impact the world around us with simple acts of kindness and unwavering trust in God's goodness. Let us carry this lesson forward, seeking opportunities to serve and support one another, knowing that in doing so, we participate in the unfolding story of God's grace and love.

Deeper Insight

Reflect on how the Shunammite Woman opened her home and built a room for Elisha without expecting anything in return. Are there ways you can create space, whether literally or figuratively, for others in your life to feel welcome and cared for? Her faith in seeking Elisha after her son's death was remarkable. Can her determination encourage or inspire you to trust God in your times of crisis? Do you turn to God in times of grief or struggle, believing He can bring restoration? Does her story remind you that God is present even in life's most challenging moments? Are you willing to trust God's plan, even when it seems unclear? Are there blessings you've overlooked or taken for granted in your life? Is there a step of faith you need to take to pursue God's help or provision?

Final Thoughts

The Shunammite woman's life teaches us to embrace generosity, act with bold faith, and trust God in every season. She gave selflessly without expecting anything in return, and God blessed her abundantly. Her story reminds us that God's faithfulness remains steadfast even in moments of great challenge or scarcity. Her unwavering trust encourages us to seek Him boldly, give selflessly, and believe in His power to restore what's been lost. Her story also reminds me that faith isn't passive—it's active, courageous, and sometimes messy.

Her story also reminds me that sometimes, God's power shines the brightest in our most vulnerable moments. It challenges me to consider: Am I open enough to seek help and to trust that God will provide, even when I feel I have nothing left to give?

The Shunammite woman's life is a testament to the transformative power of faith, generosity, and perseverance. Her actions—stepping out in love and taking bold steps in times of despair—offer a timeless reminder that no matter how dire our circumstances may seem, God is always at work, ready to bring restoration and hope. I hope her example inspires you to trust God deeply, serve generously, and never underestimate the impact of a faithful heart.

Reflections on Wisdom and Understanding

As we close this chapter on wisdom and understanding, reflect on how wisdom and understanding are more than just knowledge. They are about seeing clearly, choosing wisely, and trusting deeply. While the examples of the Queen of Sheba and the Shunammite woman are very different, they both demonstrate what it means to seek truth, act with discernment, and walk in faith. The stories of both women reveal the power of a heart that pursues wisdom.

Like the Queen of Sheba seeking wisdom and building bridges through respect and generosity or the Shunammite woman through faith and perseverance, God inspires us to live with open hearts, faith, and unwavering hope. Their stories remind us that God is always faithful, present, and working for our good.

CONCLUSION: EMBRACING THE JOURNEY OF FAITH

As we conclude Volume 1 of *Exploring the Lives of Women in the Bible: Faith-Building Insights and Practical Lessons Anyone Can Use for Today's Challenges*, I hope you feel inspired, encouraged, and enriched by the remarkable stories we've explored thus far together. These women's lives reveal timeless lessons of faith, courage, love, and resilience that remain deeply relevant today.

Through these pages, we've encountered women who trusted God in moments of uncertainty — like Sarah, who waited patiently (and sometimes impatiently) for God's promises to unfold. We've met women who stood firm in their convictions — like Shiphrah and Puah, who bravely defied injustice to protect innocent lives. We've witnessed powerful examples of sacrificial love — like Rizpah, who kept vigil out of unwavering devotion to her sons. And we've seen wisdom shine through the bold actions of women like Deborah, Jael, and the Queen of Sheba.

But these stories are not isolated lessons; they are part of a larger journey that continues into Volume 2. As you reflect on the insights gained from these amazing women, consider how these lessons apply to your own life. Their faith, perseverance, and wisdom offer a roadmap for navigating challenges, embracing God's promises, and stepping boldly into your purpose.

Exploring the Lives of Women in the Bible: Faith-Building Insights and Practical Lessons Anyone Can Use for Today's Challenges Volume 2 will continue this journey, diving deeper into stories of redemption, transformation, and spiritual strength. Women like Rahab, Mary Magdalene, and Lydia will inspire us with their resilience and unwavering belief in God's power to redeem and renew. We will also uncover lessons in leadership, mentorship, and devotion that are as impactful now as they were thousands of years ago.

If there's one thing I hope you carry with you from this first volume, it's that your story matters. Just like the women we've studied, your life — with its challenges, joys, and uncertainties — is part of God's greater plan. He meets us in the wilderness like Hagar, gives us the wisdom to lead like Deborah, and blesses our faithful acts, no matter how small, like the Widow's Mite.

As you continue into Volume 2, may you walk with renewed confidence, knowing that God, who guided these remarkable women so long ago, is still working in your life today. The lessons continue, the insights deepen, and the invitation to grow in faith remains open.

I look forward to continuing this journey with you.

With gratitude and encouragement,

Hope

WE'D LOVE YOUR HONEST REVIEW!

Dear Reader,

Thank you for joining me on this journey through the foundational stories of women in the Bible—women who trusted God in uncertain times, led with courage, and embraced love in its many forms. I hope their lives strengthened your faith and offered insight into the challenges you face today.

If this book inspired or encouraged you, would you consider leaving an **honest** review on Amazon? Your words help others discover these timeless lessons and may encourage others seeking spiritual growth or support.

Even a brief review makes a difference—and I'm so grateful for your voice and presence in this community of readers.

With heartfelt thanks,

Hope Maren

Author of *Exploring the Lives of Women in the Bible: Volume 1*

GLOSSARY

Glossary

A

- **Adulterous Woman**: A woman brought before Jesus by religious leaders, accused of adultery. Jesus responded with compassion, teaching about grace and forgiveness (John 8:1-11).
- **Advocate**: One who speaks, defends, or pleads on behalf of another. Women like **The Daughters of Zelophehad** and **Phoebe** demonstrated advocacy by standing for justice and truth.
- **Anna**: A prophetess who recognized Jesus as the Messiah when He was presented at the temple (Luke 2:36-38).
- **Apostle**: A messenger chosen to spread the teachings of Jesus. **Mary Magdalene** is often called the "Apostle to the Apostles" for her role in announcing Jesus' resurrection.
- **Apocrypha:** A collection of ancient books included in some biblical traditions, particularly in Catholic and

Orthodox Bibles, but not part of the Hebrew Bible. These writings include stories of women like Judith, Susanna, and additions to Esther.

B

- **Bathsheba**: Wife of King David and mother of Solomon. Despite scandal, her story reveals redemption and God's ability to work through broken situations (2 Samuel 11; 1 Kings 1).
- **Bethulia:** A city mentioned in the *Book of Judith*, where the people relied on God's intervention during an Assyrian siege. Judith played a courageous role in this story.
- **Bible Translations**: Different versions of the Bible that vary in language style and interpretation. The **NIV**, **KJV**, and **ESV** each offer distinct approaches to conveying Scripture.
- **Boldness**: Courage to take action despite fear or uncertainty, modeled by women like **Deborah**, **Jael**, and **Ruth**.

C

- **Canaanite Woman**: A persistent mother who sought Jesus' healing for her daughter, demonstrating unwavering faith (Matthew 15:21-28).
- **Covenant**: A sacred agreement between God and His people, often reflecting His promise of faithfulness and protection.
- **Compassion**: A deep awareness of and response to the suffering of others, modeled by **Dorcas**, **The Samaritan Woman**, and **Priscilla**.

D

- **Deborah**: A judge and prophetess known for her wisdom, leadership, and courage during Israel's oppression (Judges 4-5).
- **Disciple:** A follower or student of Jesus. Mary Magdalene is recognized as one of Jesus' most devoted disciples, present at His crucifixion and the first witness to His resurrection.
- **Diligence**: Consistent and earnest effort, modeled by women like the **Proverbs 31 Woman** and **Ruth**.

E

- **Elizabeth**: Mother of John the Baptist who praised God for His faithfulness and displayed deep joy in God's promises (Luke 1:39-45).
- **ESV (English Standard Version):** A modern English translation of the Bible first published in 2001 by Crossway. The ESV aims for word-for-word accuracy while maintaining clarity in contemporary language. Known for its literary beauty and theological precision, the ESV is widely used for personal study, teaching, and
- **Eternal Life**: The gift of everlasting life through Jesus Christ, promised to those who believe (John 3:16).
- **Eve**: The first woman created by God, whose story highlights both the consequences of sin and God's grace (Genesis 3).

F

- **Faithfulness**: Steadfast devotion to God, modeled by countless women like **Hannah**, **Mary**, and **Ruth**.

- **Forgiveness**: God's grace extended to those who repent, as demonstrated in Jesus' interaction with the **Adulterous Woman** (John 8).

G

- **Grace**: God's unmerited favor, revealed through stories like the **Adulterous Woman** and **Mary Magdalene**.
- **Good News**: The message of Jesus Christ's salvation, shared by women like **The Samaritan Woman** and **Mary Magdalene**.

H

- **Hagar**: A servant of Sarah who fled into the wilderness, where God revealed Himself as "The God Who Sees Me" (Genesis 16).
- **Healing**: Restoration of the body, mind, or spirit, as seen in the stories of the **Woman with the Issue of Blood**, the **Widow of Zarephath**, and **Dorcas**.
- **Hospitality:** The practice of generously welcoming others, often seen as a spiritual virtue. Women like Lydia and the Shunammite Woman are remembered for their hospitality.

I

- **Integrity:** The quality of being honest and morally upright. Susanna's unwavering commitment to truth in the face of false accusations highlights this virtue.
- **Intercession**: The act of praying on behalf of another, as demonstrated by women like **Hannah** and **Rizpah**.

J

- **Judgment:** In a biblical context, judgment refers to God's righteous assessment of human actions. The Wise Woman of Abel demonstrated wisdom in guiding her city away from unnecessary judgment and violence.
- **Judith:** A courageous Jewish widow who saved her people through strategic action and unwavering faith.
- **Justice:** Upholding what is fair and right, as demonstrated by the **Daughters of Zelophehad** and the **Wise Woman of Abel**.

K

- **Kindness:** An expression of God's love, modeled by women like **Ruth**, who selflessly cared for Naomi.
- **KJV (King James Version):** A traditional English translation of the Bible, completed in 1611. Known for its poetic language and influence on Christian thought and literature.

L

- **Loyalty:** Devotion and steadfast commitment, seen in relationships like Ruth's to Naomi and Mary's to Jesus.
- **Living Waters:** A metaphor for the life-giving power of Jesus Christ, used by Jesus in His conversation with the **Samaritan Woman** (John 4:10).
- **Lydia:** A successful merchant and early supporter of the Christian church, known for her hospitality and faith (Acts 16:14-15).

M

- **Mary Magdalene**: A follower of Jesus who witnessed His resurrection and was called "Apostle to the Apostles" (John 20:11-18).
- **Mentorship**: Providing guidance and support to others in their faith journey, as seen in **Priscilla**, **Eunice**, and **Lois**.
- **Messiah:** The promised Savior in Jewish and Christian belief. Mary, the mother of Jesus, played a central role in God's plan to bring the Messiah into the world.
- **Midrash:** A Jewish form of biblical interpretation that seeks to explain, expand, or explore the meaning behind Scripture. Rebekah's story is often examined in midrashic texts.

N

- **Naomi**: A widow who found renewed purpose through her relationship with Ruth and God's provision (Ruth 1-4).
- **NIV (New International Version):** A modern English translation of the Bible, first published in 1978. The NIV is known for its balance of readability and accuracy, widely used in churches and Bible study.

O

- **Obedience**: A faithful response to God's direction, modeled by women like **Zipporah**, **Deborah**, and **Mary, Mother of Jesus**.

P

- **Patriarchal Culture:** A societal structure in which men hold primary authority. Many women of the Bible, like Deborah, Esther, and Judith, demonstrated remarkable leadership despite the patriarchal norms of their time.
- **Phoebe**: A deacon in the early church, commended by Paul for her faithful service (Romans 16:1-2).
- **Perseverance**: Continuing steadfastly in faith despite hardships, as seen in **Ruth**, **Rahab**, and **Mary Magdalene**.
- **Prophetess:** A female prophet — a woman called by God to deliver His messages. Huldah, Deborah, and Anna are powerful examples of prophetesses in Scripture.

R

- **Rahab**: A woman of courage who protected Israelite spies and became part of Jesus' lineage (Joshua 2).
- **Ruth**: A Moabite woman whose loyalty, love, and faithfulness led to her place in Jesus' lineage (Ruth 1-4).
- **Redemption:** The act of being saved or restored by God's grace. Rahab's story illustrates how God's mercy transformed her life and brought her into the family line of Jesus.
- **Resilience:** The ability to endure hardship and remain steadfast in faith. Women like Tamar, Ruth, and Mary of Bethany displayed remarkable resilience in the face of trials.
- **Restoration:** The process of being renewed or returned to wholeness. The Shunammite Woman's story beautifully illustrates God's power to restore what has been lost.

- **Resurrection**: The rising of Jesus Christ from the dead, symbolizing victory over sin and death (Luke 24:1-7).

S

- **Sacrifice:** A surrender of something valuable for a greater purpose. Jochebed's courageous act of placing her infant son, Moses, in the Nile was an act of selfless sacrifice that shaped Israel's future.
- **Sarah**: The wife of Abraham, who trusted God's promise despite years of waiting (Genesis 21).
- **Sacrificial Giving**: Giving generously, as modeled by the **Widow's Mite** (Mark 12:41-44).
- **Servanthood:** A heart posture of humility and willingness to serve others. Phoebe, a servant (deacon) in the early church, modeled this beautifully.
- **Shekinah:** A term describing God's divine presence dwelling among His people. Miriam's role in leading worship after the Israelites crossed the Red Sea reflects an awareness of God's presence.
- **Steadfastness:** Unwavering loyalty and faithfulness to God. Ruth's devotion to Naomi and Mary Magdalene's loyalty to Jesus illustrate this quality.

T

- **Torah**: The first five books of the Hebrew Bible (A (Genesis, Exodus, Leviticus, Numbers, Deuteronomy), foundational to Jewish law and teachings. Women like Sarah, Rebekah, and Leah are central figures in Torah narratives.

V

- **Virtue:** Moral excellence and upright character. The Proverbs 31 Woman embodies a life of virtue rooted in wisdom, strength, and compassion.

W

- **Widow of Zarephath**: A woman who trusted God's provision during a drought and experienced miraculous provision (1 Kings 17:8-16).
- **Wisdom**: The ability to apply knowledge and understanding in God-honoring ways, demonstrated by the **Queen of Sheba** and the **Wise Woman of Abel**.

Z

- **Zipporah**: The wife of Moses who acted courageously to protect her family (Exodus 4:24-26).

This expanded glossary is designed to help readers connect with the powerful themes, key terms, and remarkable women explored in both volumes. These concepts will help you reflect on how these lessons apply to your faith journey.

UNDERSTANDING BIBLE TRANSLATIONS

E SV (English Standard Version)

A modern English translation of the Bible first published in 2001 by Crossway. The ESV aims for word-for-word accuracy while maintaining clarity in contemporary language. Known for its literary beauty and theological precision, the ESV is widely used for personal study, teaching, and preaching.

KJV (King James Version)

A traditional English translation of the Bible, completed in 1611. Known for its poetic language and influence on Christian thought and literature.

NIV (New International Version)

A modern English translation of the Bible, first published in 1978. The NIV is known for its balance of readability and accuracy, widely used in churches and Bible study.

Bible Translation Table

Translation	Style	Published	Strengths	Challenges
KJV (King James Version)	Formal, poetic, and majestic language	1611	Rich in tradition and historical influence; widely respected for its beauty and rhythm	Archaic language may be challenging for modern readers
NIV (New International Version)	Balanced between word-for-word and thought-for-thought translation	1978 (Updated in 2011)	Clear, readable language; ideal for devotional reading and public teaching	Some readers prefer a more literal translation for detailed study
ESV (English Standard Version)	Formal, word-for-word translation with modern clarity	2001	Combines accuracy with readability; popular for study, teaching, and preaching	May feel more academic or technical for casual readers

Note on Bible Translations and Their Impact

When exploring the lives of women in the Bible, the choice of translation can significantly shape the reader's understanding and reflection. Each version brings unique strengths that enhance key themes in Scripture:

- **KJV (King James Version):** The KJV's majestic language adds a sense of **reverence** and **spiritual depth** to narratives. Passages like Mary's song of praise (Luke 1:46-55) or Ruth's declaration of loyalty (Ruth 1:16-17) are especially powerful in this poetic style, making themes of devotion and worship deeply moving.
- **NIV (New International Version):** The NIV's clear, accessible language allows readers to connect with the **emotional depth** and **practical lessons** within each story. For example, the struggles of Naomi's grief, Hannah's heartfelt prayer, or the Samaritan woman's conversation with Jesus are presented with clarity, making the stories relatable to modern readers.

- **ESV (English Standard Version):** The ESV's balance of **word-for-word precision** and modern language makes it ideal for uncovering **historical insights** and **theological depth**. Stories like Esther's courageous advocacy or the wisdom of the Proverbs 31 Woman gain richness through the ESV's detailed translation.

By drawing from these translations, readers can appreciate both the **emotional heart** and **theological depth** of the women's stories explored in this book. Whether readers prefer the poetic language of the KJV, the practical clarity of the NIV, or the precision of the ESV, each translation provides meaningful insights that connect timeless biblical lessons to the challenges of today.

RECOMMENDED RESOURCES FOR
YOUR FAITH JOURNEY

As you continue your journey of faith beyond these pages, I encourage you to explore these online communities and resources. Each one offers practical tools, meaningful connections, and spiritual encouragement to help you grow deeper in your walk with God.

Love God Greatly

Website: lovegodgreatly.com

Love God Greatly exists to equip women with Bible study resources that are simple yet deeply impactful. Their free resources include printable reading plans, devotionals, and study materials translated into multiple languages. Love God Greatly also offers online study groups, giving you the opportunity to connect with other women around the world as you study God's Word together. Whether you're seeking structured Bible study or a supportive community of women walking alongside you, Love God Greatly empowers you to deepen your faith and experience God's truth in your everyday life.

Christian Women's Corner

Website: christianwomenscorner.com

Christian Women's Corner is a warm and welcoming space designed to encourage women in their spiritual growth. The site offers insightful articles, devotionals, and Bible study resources that speak directly to the challenges and questions many women face today. Whether you're seeking guidance in your relationships, prayer life, or personal faith journey, Christian Women's Corner provides practical wisdom and spiritual encouragement to help you walk confidently in God's purpose.

Other Valuable Resources for Spiritual Growth

She Reads Truth

Website: shereadstruth.com

She Reads Truth offers beautifully designed Bible studies, reading plans, and devotionals designed to engage women in Scripture daily. Their resources blend thoughtful reflection with vibrant community, encouraging you to discover how God's Word applies to your life.

Proverbs 31 Ministries

Website: proverbs31.org

Proverbs 31 Ministries provides resources that equip women to apply biblical truth to every aspect of their lives. Their devotionals, podcast series, and online Bible studies are filled with practical insights for navigating everyday challenges with wisdom and faith.

Encouragement Café

Website: encouragementcafe.com

Encouragement Café offers devotionals, podcasts, and prayer resources designed to uplift and inspire women. This supportive online community fosters connection and encouragement, helping you face life's challenges with renewed strength.

Women Living Well

Website: womenlivingwell.org

Women Living Well offers Bible studies, practical insights for balancing faith and family, and resources for creating a strong spiritual foundation. It's a wonderful resource for women seeking to thrive in their walk with God.

(In)Courage

Website: incourage.me

(In)Courage is an online community where women share stories of faith, struggle, and hope. Their devotionals and articles are designed to remind you that you are never alone — God's love is present in every season of your journey.

IF:Gathering

Website: ifgathering.com

IF:Gathering is a movement designed to equip women to grow in their faith and empower them to share Jesus with others. Their resources include small group materials, conferences, and video content that challenge and encourage women to live boldly in their faith.

Facebook Groups:

- **Women's Ministry Toolbox Community**: A group for Christian women serving in their local churches as women's ministry team leaders, Bible study leaders, or small group facilitators.
- **Christian Women Advice & Friends**: A supportive community where women can seek advice, share experiences, and participate in Bible studies.
- **Girls After Truth**: A safe space for young Christian women to connect, discuss relevant topics, and encourage each other in their faith journeys.
- **Joytime Sisters Bible Study Group**: A group for women who love Jesus and want to grow their faith, offering Bible study sessions and live video teachings.
- **Christian Women Connect**: A community aimed at inspiring, encouraging, and celebrating women, while providing prayer support and discipleship opportunities.

Online Communities and Websites:

- **She Reads Truth**: An online community committed to reading God's Word together, offering daily Bible reading plans and devotionals.
- **Good Morning Girls**: An organization that inspires, encourages, and equips women worldwide to get into God's Word through structured Bible studies and supportive online groups.
- **Aglow International**: An interdenominational organization of Christian women and men, offering local group meetings, Bible studies, and various ministry opportunities worldwide.
- **Beliefnet**: A Christian lifestyle website featuring editorial content related to inspiration, spirituality, health, wellness, love, family, news, and entertainment.
- **Pray.com**: A Christian social networking service and mobile application designed to facilitate religious communities, offering features like daily prayers, sermons, biblical content, and podcasts.
- **LoveRealm**: A Christian social networking platform providing a space for mentorship, sharing prayer requests, and connecting with other believers.

Encouragement for Continued Growth

These platforms offer various opportunities to connect with other believers. Your faith journey is personal, yet you are never alone. The beauty of today's digital world is that you can connect with like-minded women, build friendships, and grow spiritually no matter where you are. These resources are tools designed to support you — whether you're seeking deeper Bible study, meaningful conversation, or encouragement during challenging seasons. Each offers unique opportunities to connect with others, reflect on God's Word, and discover how your faith can shape your everyday life.

If you desire structured Bible study, **Love God Greatly** and **She Reads Truth** provide easy-to-follow reading plans and devotionals to help you engage with God's Word. If you're looking for inspiration, practical wisdom, or daily encouragement, **Proverbs 31 Ministries**, **Christian Women's Corner**, and **Encouragement Café** offer powerful insights designed to strengthen your faith. For those seeking deeper connections, platforms like **(In)Courage** and **IF:Gathering** foster supportive, Christ-centered conversations that remind you of God's presence in every season of life.

I encourage you to explore these communities, ask questions, and build relationships with others who are also pursuing God's truth. Just as the women we've studied throughout this book found strength in their faith, may you continue to discover the courage, purpose, and hope that God has planted within you.

Wherever you are in your journey — whether you feel strong in your faith or are searching for answers — these resources are here to remind you that **you are seen, you are valued, and you are never alone.** God's love continues to unfold in your life, and there's a community of women ready to walk this path with you. Remember, God sees you and loves you, just as you are.

Your journey isn't over — it's just beginning. 🩶

REFERENCES

Andrews University Seminary Studies. (2003). The role of Abigail in 1 Samuel 25. https://www.andrews.edu/library/car/cardigital/Periodicals/AUSS/2003-1/2003-1-04.pdf

Bible Gateway. (n.d.). Bible Gateway. https://www.biblegateway.com/

Bible Odyssey. (n.d.). Cultural exchange in the Ancient Near East. https://ww.bibleodyssey.org/articles/cultural-exchange-in-the-ancient-near-east/

Britannica. (n.d.). Deborah: Judge, prophet & leader of Israel. https://www.britannica.com/biography/Deborah-biblical-figure

Britannica. (n.d.). Queen of Sheba: Legend, history, name, & meaning. https://www.britannica.com/biography/Queen-of-Sheba

Christianity.com. (n.d.). The story of Deborah: Wisdom and leadership in times of crisis. https://www.christianity.com/wiki/bible/the-story-of-deborah.html

Christianity.com. (n.d.). What is the significance of Hannah's prayer?. https://www.christianity.com/wiki/bible/what-is-the-significance-of-hannahs-prayer.html

Christianity Today. (2023, April). Eve's legacy: Sin, redemption, and the mother of all. https://www.christianitytoday.com/2023/04/eve-legacy-sin-redemption-mother-genesis/

Divine UK. (n.d.). Transcribed talks on Mother Mary - Fr Joseph Edattu VC. https://www.divineuk.org/articles/transcribed-talks-on-mother-mary-how-did-mother-mary-overcome-her-faith-crisis-fr-joseph-edattu-vc/

Epstein, R. (n.d.). Miriam's legacy of leadership. The Jewish Theological Seminary. https://www.jtsa.edu/torah/miriams-legacy-of-leadership/

Enter the Bible. (n.d.). 2 Kings 8:1-6 – Restoring the Shunammite Woman's Property. https://enterthebible.org/passage/2-kings-81-6-restoring-the-shunammite-womans-property

Faithward. (n.d.). Hagar: The woman who named God | Genesis 16, 21. https://www.faithward.org/women-of-the-bible-study-series/hagar-the-woman-who-named-god/

Glad Tidings Magazine. (2016, August). Sarah: Faith in God's promises. https://gladtidingsmagazine.org/wp-content/uploads/2017/07/Art6.Aug2016-Sarah-Faith-in-Gods-Promises.pdf

GotQuestions.org. (n.d.). What is the significance of Hannah's prayer?. https://www.gotquestions.org/Hannahs-prayer.html

GotQuestions.org. (n.d.). What is the story of David and Michal?. https://www.gotquestions.org/David-and-Michal.html

Groundwork Online. (n.d.). Ruth: Love and faith in action. https://groundworkonline.com/blog/ruth-love-and-faith-in-action

King James Bible Online. (n.d.). Apocrypha Books. https://www.kingjamesbibleonline. org/Apocrypha-Books/

Lifeway Research. (n.d.). Lifeway Research. https://research.lifeway.com/

Ligonier Ministries. (n.d.). The widow's sacrificial contribution. Reformed Bible. https:// www.ligonier.org/learn/devotionals/widows-sacrificial-contribution

Love God Greatly. (n.d.). Encouragement and Bible study resources for women. https:// lovegodgreatly.com/

Martin, B. (n.d.). Characteristics we can learn from Moses' courageous mother. Cross-walk.com. https://www.crosswalk.com/family/parenting/characteristics-we-can-learn-from-moses-courageous-mother.html

Reformed Bible. (n.d.). The widow's sacrificial contribution. https://www.ligonier.org/ learn/devotionals/widows-sacrificial-contribution

The Bible Project. (n.d.). Explaining biblical themes like Covenants, Sacrificial Giving, and Redemption. https://bibleproject.com/

Theology of Work Project. (n.d.). Shiphrah and Puah: Two Ezer midwives defy the king. https://www.theologyofwork.org/key-topics/women-and-work-in-the-old-testa ment/shiphrah-and-puah-two-ezer-midwives-defy-the-king-exodus-18-22/

TheologyofWork.org. (n.d.). The role of women in faith and leadership. https://www. theologyofwork.org/

The BAS Library. (n.d.). Rachel and Leah. https://library.biblicalarchaeology.org/arti cle/rachel-and-leah/

www.ingramcontent.com/pod-product-compliance
Lightning Source LLC
Chambersburg PA
CBHW031531120626
46545CB00005B/2096